Carriage 451

by Barry Joyce

Author's note

My mother knew Joseph Boyle when she was a young girl. He would call with a mutual friend at my Grandparent's house and over dinner would recall tales of their exploits in the Yukon gold rush and later in the first world war. She would recount many of them to us kids and it was almost inevitable that I would investigate this extraordinary man, if only to find out whether the stories were true. They are, along with many others.

Copyright © 2023 B V Joyce

Prologue

On 29th October 1888, Russia's Imperial train was carrying the Royal family from the Crimea to St Petersburg. The Emperor, Tsar Alexander lll, was enjoying lunch with his family in the dining car as it approached the small town of Borki in Ukraine.

But it was travelling too fast. The front wheels of the second carriage suddenly left the tracks and a domino effect swiftly rippled through the train with each carriage in turn being derailed, many of them tumbling down a steep embankment. The dining car reared up and rolled over several times, crushing the roof but mercifully coming to a rest upright. After the crashing and screeching of tortured metal had died down, an eerie silence left the impression that no one had been left alive.

The sound of a crying child finally broke the silence. It was little Olga, the family's six-year-old, who was soon calmed by comforting words from her parents who were only now stirring, surprised to find that they were still alive and beginning to test out their limbs. The Tsar was an extremely large man and had considerable difficulty moving around in the very restricted headroom. But through the clouds of dust, he spotted some rays of daylight and moved towards them, calling for the others to follow. A window had been shattered and then compressed, but the opening was extremely small, big enough for only the very smallest child to pass through.

As Alexander pondered the problem, escape from the carriage suddenly became infinitely more pressing. With the violent movements of the coach, a pan of cooking oil on the galley stove had ignited and spilt widely. The wood panelling was already alight and the whole carriage would be a furnace before long.

Poking around for inspiration, Alexander found that lifting a section of the roof provided just enough room for a person to scramble through. Quickly, he put his shoulder to the roof and called in turn to his five children, his wife and a couple of servants who were close by. It was a superhuman effort and, when they were all through and he could take the load off his back, he sat back for a while, totally exhausted. But there was no time to lose. The blaze was now crackling fiercely, with smoke making breathing increasingly difficult.

But then, as if by some miracle, Alexander watched the roof begin to lift with his wife, Maria, shouting to him to get out right now. With a new lease on life, he began to crawl through the opening but found he was still too big for it. Then, suddenly, he felt strong hands grabbing hold of his arms and begin slowly and painfully to pull him clear, with flames already licking at his feet.

The survival of the Royal Family was pronounced a miracle, but twenty-three lives were lost that day. An attractive ornate cathedral was built in the town to mark the tragedy, which became the focus of an annual pilgrimage for royalty to give thanks for their survival and to honour the dead. The last of these visits was in 1915 by Alexander's son, Tsar Nicholas II, only a couple of years before his abdication and subsequent slaughter by the Bolsheviks.

When the dust from the crash had settled, it was Alexander's wife, Empress Maria Feodorovna, who was most affected by the loss of the imperial train. Although Danish by birth, her marriage to Alexander was a popular choice and she threw herself into speaking their language and learning of their hopes and fears. Very soon, she became universally loved by the Russian people.

Leaving great matters of state to her husband, she concentrated her efforts on charitable work and the general betterment of peasant lives, tirelessly travelling across the vast country and to other parts of Europe. Long before the rise of air travel, this was the golden age of the rail and the imperial train had been wrecked. A temporary replacement was cobbled together from some of the more salvageable carriages, but Maria decided she needed something better suited to her needs.

Working around the clock on her detailed requirements, the mighty Kolomna Locomotive Works constructed her carriage which was assigned catalogue number 451.

Despite some efforts by Alexander to modernise, he maintained the autocratic rule of the Romanov dynasty and, with high taxes and harsh living conditions, unrest was widespread. The rise of Marxist groups gathered speed and revolution was in the air. To counter such threats, the carriage's body was armour-plated, formed in two thick layers of hardened steel. But the interior was afforded a treatment more appropriate for the Empress of Russia. The walls of her personal space, the reception room and bedroom were panelled in fine wood, with no expense spared on furnishing and decorations. It also included some modern luxuries, including its own electric plant for heating and lighting. It must have been the finest railway carriage in the world.

For some twenty years, she travelled comfortably in her carriage until a new, more contemporary Imperial train was provided by the State for use by the Royal family. Even so, it was with considerable reluctance that she retired the carriage and put it up for sale. After failing to find a buyer, she was eventually persuaded by its highly persuasive manager to donate it to the new Petrograd Rail Museum. And here, it could have rested on permanent public display.

But it was destined for a much more adventurous life. The world was heading inexorably towards some terrible events. The Great War would take more than two million Russian lives, followed by many more under the horrors of the Red Terror. This tale is a fictionalised account of many well-documented events. Certain locations and time frames have been modified. The principal characters were real people, with others being used to aid the narrative.

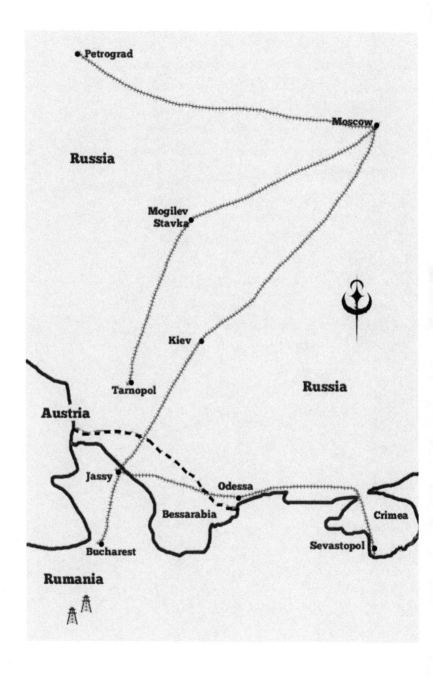

6

Chapter 1

The chatter of gunfire interrupted Joe Boyle's concentration. He had been putting the finishing touches to a report for the London office on the appalling state of morale he had found on his arrival in Petrograd. The ten days that shook the world were in the past now and the Bolsheviks were in full control of the city, but sporadic outbreaks of local violence like this still occurred from time to time.

Joe was not a man to ignore such an event. He gently laid aside his trusty Parker pen and headed towards the window, flicking off the light as he passed to avoid becoming a target. A bright half-moon lent an eerie glow to the scene. Unlike many other areas, the Revolution had been mercifully bloodless in Petrograd, but the otherwise empty boulevards of Russia's then-capital city were still littered with burned-out vehicles, breached barricades and abandoned streetcars.

A second burst of gunfire, closer this time, forced Joe to move away from the window. He looked at his watch which confirmed his stomach's reminder that it was time for dinner. From the previous night's experience, the thought failed to fill him with much enthusiasm, although he could only imagine the chef's problems, scavenging for suitable ingredients in the few local markets that survived.

Uncertain of the source of the gunfire, he slowly opened the door and peered out. The corridor was dimly lit by a few naked bulbs, but his eyes were immediately drawn to some movement on the half-landing below. A man appeared to be polishing a long knife with his handkerchief. Intrigued, Joe quietly eased the door fully open and took a stealthy pace forward from where he could see that the knife was very long, more like a sword, and it was blood that he was wiping from it.

The man suddenly sensed another presence and looked up towards Joe. For several seconds, the scene froze into a bizarre tableau, each man simply staring at the other, expecting him to make the first move.

It was Joe who finally summoned up a smile and said, 'You been having trouble?'

'As a matter of fact, I have,' The man spoke with some relief in a clear English accent. 'I was ambushed out in the street. Had to use my faithful old weapon here.' With that, he picked up a walking stick from the floor and sheathed the sword back into it. Explanation complete, he returned Joe's smile.

'You American?' he queried.

'Canadian. And you're English. Right?' As they met up on the landing and shook hands, Joe said, 'With that sort of devilish weapon, I'm glad we're on the same side.' After a moment's thought, he added, 'I'm just on my way for a spot to eat. Join me? I'd like to hear more about the attack.'

'Sure,' the Englishman agreed after only the slightest hesitation, 'and I want to know more about that fancy dress uniform you're wearing.' He smiled and then, perhaps realising that his remark might offend, he added, 'I need a few minutes. You go on down and I'll join you shortly.' After a few seconds, he added, 'Did you not see me as a threat? What would you have done if I'd run up the stairs brandishing my sword?'

'I'd have killed you,' said Joe simply.

In the dim light, it was only then that the Brit noticed the holster at Joe's waist. He just nodded. 'See you in a bit then,' he said.

The hotel's dining room oozed neglected opulence. Lit by three giant candelabras, the missing bulbs added little atmosphere to the sad sea of empty tables and chairs. Joe warily selected a table away from the windows and, as his new companion arrived, he rose and once again offered his hand with, 'I'm Joe.'

'George. George Hill.' As he looked around the room, he continued, 'I haven't eaten in here before. Is it always so crowded?

Joe replied with a smile, 'You'd be surprised. I've seen around twenty tables at times.'

They studied each other for a few moments. Joe was approaching fifty now and placed his companion a good ten years his junior. He was a good-looking young man, he thought, with jet-black hair and wearing an immaculate dark grey suit.

'I see you're not in uniform, George. You're not military then?'

'I do have a commission - rank as Captain, but I'm usually seen in civvies.'

'You're a spy then.'

George visibly jumped in his seat a tad and leaned forward, 'I'm a military adviser... attached to the British Mission.' He nodded his head towards the walls.

'Sorry,' said Joe. After a short pause, he continued, 'Now, tell me about your assailant. Did you kill him?'

'I'm not sure. He'll certainly be in a bad way. He came at me from the shadows with a knife but hesitated for just a split second as I drew my sword. That allowed me to act first and I aimed for his stomach. I think It went straight through, and he fell to the street shrieking. Again I was lucky because his mate hung back and then took fright - simply ran away.'

'Do you know what they were after?'

'Yes. Me. I don't know who they are, but I believe I know who sent them.' After a moment's thought, he continued, 'It's a long story, but I'll keep it brief. London's become increasingly concerned about keeping Russia onside, and much of my brief involves monitoring the ever-changing situation. The Revolution hasn't helped because many of the Bolshevik leaders are known to favour a ceasefire - with a number even wanting to throw their lot in with Germany. I am part of an unofficial discussion group organised by a courageous old lady who told me tonight that she thought my identity may have been compromised and that my life could be in danger. It's a source of information I'll miss, but I'll have to walk away from it now.'

The waiter, who had been chatting with other guests, came over to their table. He spoke in Russian, a language unknown to Joe, and held a lengthy conversation with George. The chef had claimed to have prepared an excellent boeuf bourguignon for tonight's meal, and would we care to order some wine. Joe had tried a glass of the local brew on his arrival a couple of days earlier and had not been impressed. Perhaps the waiter spotted this in Joe's face, 'I'll fetch the wine list. In the past, our cellar had quite a reputation. The owner hid the entrance during the Revolution to prevent looting, but he's opened it up tonight.'

The list was indeed very impressive. Joe selected a Chateau Mouton Rothschild, 'My treat,' he insisted to his blanching companion. 'I've known several Rothchilds in my time. It's time for payback.' If this sounded like name-dropping, he was simply stating a fact, for he was still in partnership with one of the Rothschilds from his previous life in the Alaskan goldfields.

The good food and fine wine were matched by the conversation, making for a highly enjoyable evening. It was to be the first of many such over the coming months, as the two men's relationship developed ever stronger. Later, they relieved the restaurant staff and took a second bottle to the lounge.

They talked of many things that first evening, George of his carefree upbringing in leafy London suburbs and of his time in Sandhurst, Joe of his years in Alaska, the fortune he'd made and his eventual unofficial title of 'King of the Klondike'. He explained how the outbreak of war in Europe had changed his outlook on life, and how he had thrown both his energies and his wealth into the Allied war effort, raising and equipping a small army and placing it at the disposal of the Canadian Expeditionary force. Following it to Europe, he was adjudged too old to fight and enlisted the help of his many influential contacts to find him a useful role. He was eventually given the monumental task of reorganizing the Russian railway system which had ground to a halt and was severely hampering the Russian war effort. That very morning, he had presented letters of introduction to the Russian Minister for Railways. Anticipating a stony reception for getting involved in their internal affairs, the Minister had proved very grateful for Joe's help and gave him a generous amount of his time.

'He introduced me to his heads of department and gave me several top-level contacts. I have an assortment of railway maps, timetables and other documents. And I also have the promise of a railway carriage for my personal use.'

If George's eyes widened at this, they very nearly popped out when Joe continued, 'and tomorrow - no, later this morning - I intend to visit the new Bolshevik HQ at the Smolny Institute.' He paused for just a moment before continuing, 'And, as you seem to have nothing better to do right now, I would really appreciate it if you would accompany me. You speak their language and I would find that very useful.'

George had not seen this coming and sat still, saying nothing. But the following morning, a few intrepid passers-by were faintly amused at the sight of the two men, both in full dress uniform, Joe with a sword buckled at his side, marching down to the Institute.

Previously a boarding school for daughters of nobility, Lenin himself had chosen to requisition this property as his headquarters. They passed through the gates without a challenge and immediately began fighting their way through the crowded courtyard. Heavily armed Red Guard soldiers and sailors, dressed frequently in tattered uniforms, were joined by a fearsome-looking bunch of volunteers who resembled Mexican bandits with a belt, sometimes two belts, full of bullets wound around their bodies. No one seemed to be in charge and they simply milled around in groups seeking some form of action.

Although no weapons were permitted inside the building, it was equally busy with all-comers being encouraged to witness a new form of open government and the demise of corrupt and secretive politics. Even so, at one point the two men found themselves challenged by armed guards controlling entry to a more secure area.

'We're here to see Comrade Joffe,' George announced.

One of the sentries recognised the name and opened a gate, idly waving them through. The maze of corridors continued, with crowded rooms on either side. George's calls for Joffe at each room were mostly ignored but occasionally elicited a wave further down the corridor. Finally, a tall dark-haired bespectacled man approached them with a smile.' I'm Joffe,' he announced. Evidently an educated man, he continued in passable English. 'Sorry if you've had difficulties finding me. Which of you is Colonel Boyle?'

Joe extended his hand. 'Sorokin told me you'd be coming in today,' said Joffe. 'I gather you've volunteered to sort out our terrible railway system. Believe me, you're very welcome.'

Joe smiled, shrugged and said, 'Anything to assist the war effort. We'll do what we can.'

'It's a wider problem than simply supplying the front, I'm afraid. We are virtually cut off here from Moscow, which is completely gummed up - the Moscow Knot they call it.'

'Well, we're going to need a little help,' said Joe. 'Some funds, for a start. And an open permit to travel throughout the country. You may be the official government now but the whole country is in turmoil, and we'll need to visit areas controlled by some very different factions.'

'Right. I can certainly help with the first, but I think you need a more powerful signature for your travel pass.' Looking around and raising his voice, 'Where's Lenin? Has anyone seen him?'

After confirmation that he had been seen in the building. Joffe ordered a couple of his men to seek him out, and another to find a typewriter and some paper. Some twenty minutes passed before the Bolshevik leader sauntered into the room surrounded by his entourage.

His familiar austere face broke into a smile as he approached Joffe and shook his hand. The smile remained as he surveyed the two men, perhaps finding their immaculate uniforms more amusing than impressive. Joffe outlined the problems being experienced by the country's railway systems, Lenin nodding occasionally. He asked a couple of searching questions, but the to and fro of the translation made for a rather tedious form of conversation and Lenin cut it short.

'I'll certainly assist where I can,' he concluded. 'Whether or not we continue with the war, we'll need our railways sorted out.

The alarming element of this statement prompted worried glances between Joe and George. Pulling out of the war was clearly on the agenda for the top brass in the new Bolshevik government.

With that, Lenin took the permit that had been prepared, perused it briefly and then signed it, passing it to Joe. At the last moment, he snatched it back and began writing under his signature, 'This is very important. Please give these two Comrades all possible help, Vladimir Lenin.'

Although unsure about their new titles, the two friends left highly content with their visit. When they arrived back at their hotel, there was a message from the Railways Minister inviting them to call at the city's main rail yard to select a suitable carriage. It turned out to be a graveyard for the once great system, a vast collection of engines, passenger coaches, goods vehicles and every conceivable item of railway paraphernalia. Some had been left to the ravages of time and weather, but others had been preserved with many of them displayed in a sizable museum, closed for the moment.

Under Joe's instruction, George asked to see the Yard manager, who turned out to be an elderly man, a true railway enthusiast now embittered by years of neglect and lack of investment in the industry. He was also an educated man and spoke a heavily accented, but understandable, form of English. Joe was quick to seize the opportunity to gain expert insight into the industry's problems, along with ideas for possible solutions. Always a prolific note-taker, Joe found himself eagerly scribbling for over an hour before the manager called a halt to his questions with, 'Now. You want a carriage I understand.'

'The Minister did promise me one,' exclaimed Joe.

'Yes. He told me. If you will leave the choice to me, I think I have the perfect one for you. Follow me.'

He led them out through a maze of sheds to a large open hangar in which several Pullman and other high-class carriages were on display, probably as part of the museum. He stopped in front of a large solid-looking example and announced proudly, 'Number 451. It was built for Empress Marie Feodorovna and it's a tank, with bullet-proof walls, but some luxuries too. Let's go up and I'll show you around.'

Almost half the carriage was given over to a large living room, with areas for dining and office work. The bedroom had a small double bed and en-suite, and there was a kitchen along with two further sleeping cabins.

'There is one further asset that comes with this carriage.' Then, after a short pause, he added, 'Ivan. He was the Empress's '*provodnik*' ever since she purchased it. And he is available, should you wish to employ him. Needless to say, he knows every inch of the carriage and could be very useful to you. I'm afraid he's not here today so I can't introduce you. He's a good man but takes a bit of getting used to. He is a fierce Royalist, honest and loyal, but I'm afraid has little sense of humour.'

'I'm sure he'll be most useful,' said Joe. 'And the carriage is ideal. Thank you very much.'

Back in the office, Joe asked if they could move in the following day as he wanted to set it up as his HQ as soon as possible. 'That's fine,' the manager agreed. 'So long as you don't grill me again about the state of the railways.'

'I'm sorry,' Joe apologised. 'I took too much of your time.'

'It's fine. I've already thought of other improvements you might consider. I'll be happy to talk some more.'

Having packed his few belongings the previous evening, Joe was up early and checked out of the hotel, regretting only the loss of his evening treat from the sunny slopes of the Gironde Estuary. The manager had already arrived and appeared to have gained a new lease of life from Joe's interest in his work, offering him another session over coffee later in the morning.

Joe spent a couple of hours settling in and was preparing for a break when a tall, elderly man swung himself nimbly up into the carriage. His gaunt face contained no semblance of a smile, and without offering a hand, he stared at Joe announcing simply, 'Ivan.' With no common language between the two men, Joe welcomed him as best he could but smartly left to meet up with the manager, who was again most generous with both his time and suggestions.

Chapter 2

Rivulets of rain cascade down the window of the small smoke-filled office. An elderly grey-haired man with a trim, matching moustache sits behind a large oak desk. He opens a file, writes briefly into it and slams it on top of another of the many piles, adding another puff of dust to the room. A knock at the door elicits a loud 'Come' from the corner of his pipe-filled mouth.

A man, too readily accepting middle age, enters and stands in front of the desk.

'Got a wire from our man in Petrograd, Mr Coldwell. Not sure what to do with it.'

Morning, Sam.' Then, after removing his pipe. 'That's Buchanan, isn't it? Sir George Buchanan.'

'Yes, Sir.'

'What's he bleating about?'

'It's an odd one, Sir. He says there's a new face in town - swaggering around in what looks like a British army uniform, but he's got an American accent. He's attending functions and having meetings with Russian top brass. Surely, Americans are not supposed to be there?

'That's right. They're not signed up for that theatre yet.'

He leans back in his chair, deep in thought. Then, with a nod towards the piece of paper in Sam's hand, 'Is that the wire?'

'Yes.'

'Hmm. Leave it with me.' He pushes the telegram to the edge of his desk.

That evening, Joe and George met up for dinner in a city centre restaurant. The events of the day dominated the conversation until a strong and bitter coffee arrived.

'The other night, Joe. You didn't tell me about that uniform you always wear. Is it standard Canadian?'

'Another time, George. Remind me. But I've got something else on my mind right now. Have you had any thoughts about what you're going to do next?'

After a moment's thought, 'Not really. I've had a few ideas, but - no, nothing definite. I think I'll visit the Smolny HQ again tomorrow.'

'Think you'll be able to persuade Lenin and the others not to give up on the Allies?'

George smiled ruefully. 'I fear not. But it does seem a good place to dig a bit more deeply into their thinking.'

'I know Britain and Russia are allies, but it's not a relationship made in heaven. Be very careful, George. These people don't pull their punches.'

'I know,' George replied simply.

Joe was silent for a few moments, thinking. 'I'll be heading south in a couple of days, George,' he began. 'I have an introduction to General Dukhonin who heads up the Russian Army at their Headquarters at Stafka. If I can gain his support, he'll surely be able to point me to the best railway people to talk to, because I do want to get started on my report.'

'Right,' acknowledged George. 'Good luck with that.'

Joe looked at his friend silently for a moment before continuing, 'Just a thought, George. The Army HQ might prove to be an equally useful environment for your investigations. I'm sure they will provide me with an interpreter, but I've rather got used to you.'

Joe's smile was as beguiling as the words themselves and George said almost immediately, 'I thought you'd never ask, Joe.'

'Well, I don't want you on board simply to translate for me. We have common goals, and I believe we can work well together.'

'Sure,' agreed George. 'I'd very much like that. But I'm not entirely a free agent, and I'll have to get the "OK" from London. I'll do that tonight.'

But the following day, George discovered that he had perhaps jumped too quickly. London was unhappy with the proposal and wanted more information about Joe, who was the subject of odd reports arriving at the Foreign Office.

Whatever his current project, Joe always liked to grab hold of it without any delay and invariably enlisted the help of top men. He had touched base with the Railways Minister and met with Joffe and Lenin. He now decided that it might help George's case if he introduced himself to the British Ambassador.

Then, with George in limbo, he decided to find out more about the Moscow knot described by Joffe, and he very soon learned the hard way. He had always held a rather blind belief in the accuracy of the printed word and the National Timetable clearly stated that the Moscow Express would depart at 2.00 PM each day and arrive in central Moscow a trifle over 4 hours later. He was not fazed by a half-hour delay in departure, but his demeanour soon moved from mild annoyance to wild anger at the loss of valuable time. Because it was nearly two days before Joe's train finally limped into a desolate little suburban station, part of Moscow's "Little Ring" of stations. After a melancholic little whistle, the engine heaved a couple of weary blasts of steam and then died.

Several coaches were standing by, but Joe managed to secure one of the few available cabs. The Revolution's battle for Moscow had been a very different affair from that in Petrograd. The Royalists had fought fiercely for every street and every building. Approaching the city centre, the results became increasingly evident with most buildings pockmarked by rifle fire or holed by heavier ordnance. Many lay in ruins and the driver had to make frequent diversions to avoid all kinds of obstructions. At one point, he was forced to flick his whip and weave his way through a mass funeral procession with wagons piled high with corpses. The freezing weather and rigour mortis combined to leave their stiff limbs sticking out over the sides and gruesome staring faces caught in the agonies of death.

The train had been very crowded and the cramped conditions had prevented any meaningful sleep, so it was an exhausted Joe that arrived at his hotel in time for dinner. The following day, the city had barely opened for business when Joe set off to make up for lost time and it was Lenin's personal endorsement of his mission that secured an immediate meeting with Moscow's top man, Valerie Muralov.

Moscow's Kommandant turned out to be something of a pink Bolshevik, disapproving of the violent spillage of royal and noble blood and the wholesale violence that ensued. The tall, dark-haired young man was impressive and Joe took to him immediately as he slowly became fully cooperative. He explained at some length how Moscow's rail problems stemmed from the almost total disaffection of railway staff at all levels. Pay had become only sporadic and, with long hours and poor conditions, men failed in droves to turn up for work. Others had become Marxist sympathisers and turned to acts of sabotage.

Joe listened with increasing apprehension. He had never underrated the likely difficulties, but sabotage added a new dimension to his task. Muralov introduced him to Moscow's chief engineer, Nicholai Vasiliev, and the three of them began to work up a campaign for action.

A couple of days later, Joe and Nicholai stood before a mass meeting of railway workers. A buzz of hostility pervaded the vast hangar in which it had been called and, with several hundred men screaming abuse, Nicholai had great difficulty in making himself heard. It had been decided that he should open the proceedings by introducing Joe as a new face, an expert brought in from abroad, who would then set out the new measures.

Joe Boyle, who knew well how to manage a large audience, took a couple of sharp steps forward, raising his arms aloft in a victory "V". This caused a brief dip in noise, sufficient for Joe to shout in his deep sonorous voice 'Friends.' The sheer volume brought a further dip and, when an animated interpreter shrieked a translation, the noise dampened down to a whisper.

'From this day forward, anyone found to be engaged in an act of sabotage will be shot.' Joe did not anticipate that such measures would ever become necessary, but he was aware that his audience was unaccustomed to idle threats and would take them at face value. Translation met with a surge of angry mutterings which Joe sought to quell as early as possible. Stepping forward once more, he started again, 'I know. I know this sounds harsh. But the country is at war, and acts of sabotage are acts of treason, and therefore fully warrant the penalty of death.'

As the sounds of discontent slowly died away, Joe paused to let the effect sink in.

'I repeat, we are at war. And even as I speak, the youth of this country is bravely fighting the German hoards on all fronts, and they are suffering. Because of our broken railway system, urgently needed relief troops are stuck in barracks, armaments are languishing in sidings, and food and vital medical supplies are running short. Nothing is getting through as it should.' He paused for several seconds.

'It is surely our task to get these vital supplies to our Comrades. Is it not?'

A rhythmic stamping began, even some tentative applause. Joe was encouraged and pressed on.

'And to mend this once great system, we need you. We cannot do it without your help. From today, we expect each one of you to turn up for work every day and to carry out your duties enthusiastically. Shift supervisors will keep a list of all men who fail to do so without good reason.' After a moment's pause, he continued, 'and every tenth man on that list will be shot.'

Oddly, this sparked only a small ripple of dissent, so Joe cracked straight on.

'We do realise you have some valid grievances and in return for your cooperation, we propose to address them without delay. I have agreed with Kommandant Muralov that funds will be made available for you all to be paid reliably every week.' This brought a flurry of cheers so that Joe, feeling now that the wind was behind him, continued with a raised voice, 'Furthermore, within two weeks, all missing back pay will be calculated and paid in full.'

More cheers and applause, but still mixed with a degree of scepticism. With all the young men fighting on the western front, these were mature men who had heard such promises many times before.

'We'll be holding other meetings,' Joe continued. 'We're seeing the coachbuilders in the sheds this afternoon, and you can be sure that damaged rolling stock will be repaired and returned to you in good time. So it's up to you now, men. You know what's wrong, and how it can be mended. Think imaginatively and work courageously. If tracks are congested, blocked by broken down wagons perhaps, just shunt them off into the fields. Clear the lines and keep to timetables. Come on, men. Let's get our great railways rolling.'

Nicholai moved up to Joe and shook his hand enthusiastically. 'Excellent, Comrade. If that doesn't get them moving ...' he said, leaving any other possible consequences unsaid. And certainly, the mood of the men had lifted as they began to move off to work with considerably more spring in their steps.

Joe remained in Moscow for a further eight days until Muralov's promises on pay had materialised and significant signs of reform had begun to be seen. It was therefore with some confidence that he mounted the return train to Petrograd and, as he sank back into the deeply upholstered first-class seat, his mind turned to a similar aggressive meeting he had experienced some twenty years earlier in Alaska.

Chapter 3

Joe Boyle was stone broke. He had spent several years touring the length of Canada promoting the heavyweight boxer, Frank Slavin, who was at one time the top contender for John L Sullivan's world heavyweight title. But time and bruising fights had taken their toll on his body and, as his popularity had waned, the two men decided to take their chances in the flourishing Yukon gold rush.

It was mid-July 1897, and the steamship from San Francisco called first at Juneau, a frontier town set amidst thousands of miles of uncharted wilderness, but which had now found a fresh life as a base from which to launch a search for the elusive treasure. It was also a wild town where all men carried weapons and murders were frequent.

Travellers to the goldfields were required to personally carry sufficient supplies for the journey and the two men had only $10 between them. Somehow, they must earn cash for tickets to Skagway on the next leg of their journey. Joe felt that a boxing match would prove popular to this seething mass of men and had posters printed promoting a 'Red hot boxing exhibition' between the world-famous Frank Slavin and 'a stout contender', who would prove to be Joe Boyle himself. Indeed, it proved very successful and they sold 100 tickets at $5 apiece.

But Juneau was administered by the US Army and, in an effort to calm the violence in the city, had issued an edict that no bare-knuckle fighting would be permitted. The hall was packed to the rafters and Joe was furious, but was eventually forced to comply. Not to be robbed so easily of his hard-earned grubstake, he leapt into the ring to address the increasingly rowdy crowd. His powerful voice soon rose above the shouting and stamping.

'Friends…Friends,' he shouted. 'You have paid good money for a night out and I, Joe Boyle, will make sure you get one.'

As the noise subsided somewhat, Joe continued. 'There's a piano on the stage and I can promise you a full programme of music, song and humour.'

In a quieter atmosphere now, with cheers mixed with a few jeers, Joe was quick to push home his advantage. 'But to start the show Frank Slavin, one-time contender for the World Heavyweight title, will demonstrate the art of bag punching…' This brought a round of applause from the sports-loving crowd encouraging Joe to clinch the deal with, '… and perhaps best of all, if any gentleman feels short-changed, we'll readily refund his money.'

As the evening progressed, the rumble of discontent gradually subsided. When Slavin began to tire Joe took over, interspersing music from the piano and his colourful baritone voice with jokes from his extensive repertoire. To deafening applause, he completed a full 90-minute programme and then, at the audience's insistence, continued for a further 20 minutes. Not one man collected his money back.

Joe had never doubted that his powerful presence could hold and win over a hostile audience. He had already used it once in Russia and would require it again - on occasions under the threat of death. The evening became the talk of the town in Juneau and he was approached by a prominent businessman, Captain William Moore, with a proposal to find a new way to the goldfields, starting from Skagway. Some early investigations had suggested that the idea might prove an easier route than the current Chilkoot Pass, a terrifying and exhausting journey with horses and men being killed every day on the Golden Staircase. With Moore's promise of equipment and provisions, along with money for teams of horses and packers to carry them, the offer was irresistible and Joe readily agreed.

Now with cash for fares and some small change for pocket money, Joe's party could continue to Skagway which proved to be a much smaller town, although just as crowded - and totally lawless.

There were no wharves or jetties from which to unload all the supplies. Hundreds of men were transporting their baggage, freight and even horses in rowing boats and canoes. Some of the equipment promised by Captain Moore was already with them, but getting it safely off boats that heaved in the foaming sea edge required strength, judgement and a degree of luck. As Joe took charge, Slavin shouted, 'Great work, Captain', alluding to a previous life of his at sea. Most characters involved in the gold rush would pick up a nickname and this title caught on. For some years, Joe was known as 'Captain' until he was eventually promoted to royalty.

Apart from the sea of tents on the beach, Skagway consisted of just a handful of wooden buildings, many of them saloons. With much of the stores now provided for, Joe discarded the notion of sleeping on the beach and followed his usual practice of renting quality accommodation. Very soon, he was settled in the best rooms in town discussing the route to the goldfields with Frank. Dawson City, standing on the Yukon river, acted as the hub for gold exploration, but it was around six hundred miles from Skagway across some of the wildest terrain imaginable, including several lakes and mountains. But first, they had to scale the range of sugarloaf peaks that border the sea, acting as a backdrop to Skagway.

When the remainder of Captain Moore's supplies arrived, Joe finalised his arrangements. He scoured the saloons of Skagway, haggling with the strongest and fittest-looking men until he had assembled a team of eighteen packers and around twenty horses. However, when Joe returned to his hotel, he found his suite locked and all his possessions packed into one of the smallest rooms imaginable. A furious Joe stormed down to reception only to be told that his rooms had been rented to a certain Mr Smith. Joe turned rapidly on his heels and set off at speed towards the staircase, clearly aiming for a confrontation, but he was stopped in his tracks by a thunderous shout from the man behind the counter.

'Just a moment, Mr Boyle.'

'Huh…' exclaimed Joe.

'Don't try to take on Soapy Smith. He'll kill you.'

'The hell he will,' Joe yelled and started once again.

'I'm serious,' the receptionist shouted so earnestly that Joe turned and stopped to hear him out. The young man beckoned him closer and began to talk softly, almost in a whisper.

'Soapy is a dangerous man. He's the boss of all crime in Skagway and owns a lot of it, even Diamond Lil's.' Then, he lowered his voice still further, 'He is utterly ruthless, Mr Boyle. He wouldn't give it a moment's thought about wiping you out - or more likely getting someone else to do it. He seems to have taken a dislike to you. He hates it when he's not the centre of attention, and you've made yourself popular with your entertainment in Juneau. The town's buzzing with it.'

Joe stopped for thought. His immediate instinct was to confront Soapy Smith but his head advised otherwise. 'Thanks for the warning,' he said to the receptionist. 'It's only one night. We'll be gone in the morning.'

The sun had already been up for an hour, warming the chill night air. Miners were loading stores into horses' large panniers and before long Joe was leading the packstring away. The first section of the White Pass trail had been open for some time and in the fine weather Joe hoped to reach the summit before the day ended. But dangerous footing, narrow gorges and boggy ground soon slowed progress and it was almost the end of the third day before they reached the summit from where Joe and his friend were able to make out Lake Linderman in the distance and beyond it, Lake Bennett.

'There she is, Frank,' said Joe. 'Our next destination. Looks like a doddle, eh?'

That afternoon, Joe took stock and then outlined his plan. 'The team will rest up for a day or two. Tomorrow, I am going on alone,' he announced. 'It'll be easier that way. I'll be travelling light, just essential supplies and a rifle - I'm sure there'll be grizzlies about. As I go, I'll leave stone markings for you to follow. Under Mr Slavin's leadership, the trail will need to be widened and improved for its more permanent use.'

One of Boyle's many unique achievements in the Yukon was the pioneering route he blazed that week. Although frequently unusable in the winter months, it became the trail of choice for thousands of gold prospectors when the rush reached its height the following year. Later, it became the preferred route for the Whitehorse and Yukon Railway. Fraught with all manner of difficulties and dangers, it took him five days and nights of almost unbroken slogging through the bush. He had a compass bearing but was frequently forced off course by the topography, with only the occasional glimpse of his goal. Even in summer, permafrost had left large areas of the waterlogged swamp, making progress slow and treacherous. He met with a variety of cul-de-sacs, gaping chasms, bodies of water, and impenetrable granite cliffs, forcing him to retrace his steps to begin the section again. And wildlife, clouds of mosquitoes would be the least of his problems for he had to be on the constant lookout for snakes in the undergrowth and bears from the trees. Every hundred yards or so, he would mark his route - a cairn of stones where they existed, notched trees, an arrow of sticks, or sometimes simply a pile of mud. It was a most remarkable feat.

Finally, Joe burst through a thicket of trees, to reveal Lake Bennett whose shores were alive with prospectors constructing boats of all sizes. Having survived the hardships they encountered on the Chilcott Pass, this leg introduced a further stern test of the men's resolve. For they now faced a long treacherous journey along a string of lakes and waterways that led to the Yukon River and their final destination, Dawson City. Those who ignored the advice to quit by the North West Mounted Police, felled their trees, cutting them into planks with long whipsaws. To get the necessary straight and true edges was a task well beyond the capability of most men, and many would drown on their journey.

Fortunately, Joe did not need to involve himself in such toil as Frank would in time arrive with Captain Moore's exhaustive supplies, which included an eight-metre collapsible boat. After a day's rest, Joe retraced his trail, improving the ground and markings until he met up again with Slavin and his party.

At Lake Bennett, it was time for the group to split and make their own way to Dawson. The two friends set off the following day with Joe at the helm. Other boats were also making an early start, some making better progress than others. A round coracle type of boat was found impossible to control and travelled in endless circles. Another began sinking almost immediately, mercifully still in shallow water.

Starting off with a punting pole was simple enough but, as the water got deeper, using the oars soon exposed their inexperience. However, they were both powerful men and fast learners so by the time they entered Lake Tagish their rhythm had substantially improved. This was just as well, as the next stretch of river was notorious and would take the lives of many men. The light was beginning to fail and Joe decided to camp for the night to recover their strength before tackling it.

As soon as they set off the following morning, the boat began to pick up speed as it entered Miles Canyon. Joe was taken by surprise and soon found himself battling against a seething torrent of water. Fierce upstands slewed the craft off course so that almost all control was lost. Joe's only hope was to keep it upright and fend off approaching rocks. At one point, they ran into the outer edges of a giant whirlpool which drew them relentlessly down into the eye of the maelstrom. The only point of exit led perilously close to the granite sides of the canyon and Joe's first attempt to break out failed. But, with his heart in his mouth, he heaved again at the tiller and the boat reared up and then re-joined the main flow only briefly scraping the rocky walls.

But the reward for this success was to be thrown into the roaring waters of the Squaw Rapids, the current's speed increasing all the time. Jagged black rocks threatened immediate disaster as Joe tried to pick a

30

safe route through the foaming water. But there was no let-up and their frightening speed continued to accelerate as they entered the narrowing walls of Whitehorse. They pitched, bucked and swung as Joe hung onto the tiller and prayed until, quite suddenly, they broke out into the quiet, sunlit basin that led into Lake Lebarge.

As they rowed to the shore to take stock, their shattered nerves were only relieved by almost uncontrollable laughter. They were still more than two hundred miles from their goal, but the worst was over. five days later, they dragged their boat up the shores of Dawson City, adding it to the many hundreds of others that had completed the journey. Their first reaction was one of disappointment. To call the collection of tents, huts and a few wooden buildings a city was nothing more than a sick joke.

But they had made it, and it would become Joe's home for the next 20 years.

Chapter 4

Sam squeezes past a tea trolley parked outside the door. It is wartime, and no biscuit accompanies the cup of tea sitting on the untouched telegram from the Petrograd Embassy.

'Just been handed another wire from Buchanan in Petrograd. He's Canadian.'

'Don't be silly. He's as English as you and me.'

'No. This odd soldier he's been on about. Apparently, he's a Colonel in the Canadian army. His name is Joseph Boyle, and he's now called on the Ambassador and presented his credentials.'

'Good,' says Coldwell as he slides the telegram from under his tea, 'I can forget about this then.'

'Well, no. Not really, Sir. The Ambassador's most unsure about the man. You'd better read this,' handing Coldwell the latest missive.

Buchanan reports a strange, almost surreal, encounter. The man had produced letters of introduction from some prominent people and then explained that he had been given the job of reviving the broken Russian railway system. He had gone on to describe the last twenty years that he had spent mining for gold in the Yukon.

'It may have made him a rich man, but hardly suits him for this mammoth task.' The telegram continues, 'And now the blighter's gone off to Moscow. Who is sponsoring him? Who controls his actions? With no experience in diplomacy, he's in danger of becoming a loose cannon. Please inform and advise.'

Coldwell takes a long slug of tea and then makes up his mind. 'Buchanan says he's Canadian, doesn't he? I think we can safely pass this matter on to the Colonial Office, eh?'

He passes the telegram back. 'Arrange that will you, Sam.'

George was there to meet Joe at Petrograd station. It made him realise how much he had missed his new friend and how well they complemented each other. Joe was aware that he could be considered a trifle headstrong. He was always quick to size up any situation, but his natural reflex was to take immediate, sometimes precipitous, action. George, he thought, was more likely to pause for greater consideration, although this may occasionally lose vital initiative.

As they made their way back to Carriage 451, George announced that he had received a somewhat reluctant nod from London to permit him to work alongside Joe, but it was full of conditions.

'Don't worry about them, George.' Said Joe, closing any more discussion on the subject. He was very pleased to have George on board.

'I have been hearing stories of problems at Army HQ,' said George.

'That's right,' agreed Joe, 'I gather Lenin and Trotsky have been actively drawing up plans for peace between Russia and Germany - the last thing we want to hear.'

He pauses for a moment. 'We should go to Stavka, George. We may be able to do something!'

'Agreed,' said George, and waited a few seconds before continuing. 'Incidentally, that uniform of yours. You never told me about it the other night.'

'Not now, George. I've got a lot of reports to write up.'

Left to his own, George's thoughts began to echo the reflections of his friend. He had been delighted with Joe's suggestion that they should team up - both delighted and a trifle flattered, for he had detected in Joe a man of considerable stature.

Certainly, he could not match his physical strength or stamina. The man was built like an ox, with muscles trained to peak as a heavyweight boxer. But over the next few months, he would observe Joe in many often perilous, situations and his enigmatic character would gradually emerge.

Above all, he was his own man. Nothing was allowed to get in the way of any action he considered to be right. His adventurous spirit, which had led him in his teens to run away to sea, forced him to seek out wherever the action was. This resulted in long periods away from home rendering his private life a shambles, including at least two disastrous marriages. Serious, with a strong work ethic, he could also be very entertaining, with a fund of humour and a fine singing voice. And with his skilled oratory, he would also delight in recounting tales of his exploits, rarely neglecting to embellish them to his advantage.

He was indeed a most powerful personality. George later wrote in his memoirs, "Such was Colonel Boyle, a man whose equal I have encountered neither before or since, and to have enjoyed his friendship and to have worked under and with him, will always remain one of the proudest memories of my life."

The following day, the Yard manager called early on George and Joe in Carriage 451 as he had agreed for it to be hitched to the midday train going south. But he arrived with bad news. General Dukhonin, chief of the Russian Army, for whom Joe had a letter of introduction, had fallen out with the Bolshevik hierarchy by refusing to order a ceasefire whilst peace talks between Russia and Germany continued. His brave stance, which was so important to the Allied cause, reinforced Joe's resolve to get to him as soon as possible.

In the early evening, the train stopped at Orsha and their carriage was uncoupled to await the delayed arrival of the onward train towards Stavka. The station had been overrun by groups of Bolsheviks, many of them previously soldiers still wearing their uniforms. They were a sorry sight, huddled around makeshift fires on the platforms, living off whatever meagre rations they happened to have on them.

And they brought further bad news about General Dukhonin. He had been sacked by Stalin and replaced by a junior officer, Ensign Krylenko, who was also heading for the Stavka headquarters with a crowd of Bolshevik rebels. Any sleep that was managed that night was shattered by the arrival of the Stavka train in the early hours, and it was approaching noon before the train slowly nosed into a siding at Stavka.

The station platforms had been overrun by a seething mass of Revolutionary humanity, shouting and gesticulating in the direction of the only other train in the station. No one paid much attention to Joe's train as it slowly hissed to a halt, but most of its passengers rushed to join the throng. 'Dukhonin. Dukhonin. We want Dukhonin,' they chanted, stamping their feet. There was no sign of the General, but Joe became increasingly fearful that some terrible spectacle was about to be played

35

out in front of them. He moved away from the window but, as he started for the door, George grabbed his arm.

'No, Joe,' he said quietly, but firmly. 'You can't take on a thousand men. I have seen crowds like this and there's simply no stopping them, I promise you.'

Joe hesitated, for to do nothing was against all his instincts. He knew George was right though, and said nothing but moved back to the window to await events. He did not have to wait long as a tall, lanky man appeared at the entrance to the other coach. Resplendent in full dress uniform, with banks of medals decorating his chest, he was nevertheless not the man that the rebel throng wanted to see and they continued their calls for Dukonin. The man's vain attempts to make himself heard were instantly met by boos and angry shouts and, when the more adventurous insurgents attempted to mount the train, he scurried back into the safety of the carriage.

The stamping and shouting rose to a fever pitch, but it was still several minutes before Dukonin finally appeared. A small man, with rat-like features and a cap at least two sizes too large, he kept looking back helplessly as hands could be seen pushing him roughly forward. It was impossible to tell whether these hands were treacherous or simply fearful of being overrun, but the General was clearly being offered as a sacrificial cow. When he reached the entrance, he stood still for a few moments, staring defiantly at individuals close by him. But they would not be cowed and, when he later attempted to command silence by dramatically throwing his arms wide and lifting his gaze to engage the whole crowd, the noise simply increased.

They were completely out of control now, like slavering wolves baying for blood. Joe and George remained at the window, fearful of watching but unable to turn away. The action then moved swiftly towards its inexorable end. Unable to argue his cause, Dukhonin's head dropped and, with his arms hanging limply by his side, he cut a sad and lonely figure. The Commander-in-Chief of the whole Russian Army, some five million souls, was bowing to the inevitable and surrendering his life. He seemed not to notice the hands grabbing hold of his ankles, but he soon disappeared from view as he was pulled from the platform.

In no time he reappeared, thrown high into the air between groups of rioters. This was not enough for many who soon raised the level of torment. Bayonets were fixed to rifles and held like giant pincushions for the General's body to fall onto. Gunshots too were heard and Joe, who had been forced to look away by this point, prayed to God that they were not merely being fired into the air and that Dukhonin was hopefully already dead.

When the crowd eventually tired of this, the General was left on the ground, allowing others the opportunity to thrust their bayonets into his shredded body. Very slowly, their appetite for this cruelty satisfied, the mob began to disperse and move into the nearby town, only to cause more trouble in the local taverns. As the men passed by Carriage 451, Joe peered at their faces, curious to see what sort of person would indulge in such horrific bloodshed.

A few men stayed longer, standing in an ever-growing pool of blood to plunge their bayonets into the General's dead body. Eventually, a couple of brave railway workers ended the horror by dragging the corpse into one of the engine sheds and locking it up.

Both men sat for a while, utterly drained, staring out of the window. Without looking at Joe, George took his hand and squeezed it gently. Joe turned to look at him and managed to raise a wry smile.

'I can't leave it like this, George. I have to do something.'

He got up, went to the door and climbed down from the carriage. Giving the lake of blood a wide passage, he strode towards the other train, stopping at the fateful platform from which Dukhonin had been dragged. George, aware that Joe would probably need an interpreter, drew up to his side and they entered the carriage together.

It was dark inside and crowded. 'Who's in charge here?' Joe demanded noisily. This silenced the room sufficiently for George's translation, whereupon the throng parted to reveal a slim young man seated at a large table. Wearing fatigues and a simple open white shirt, he looked up and said, 'Krylenko. Who the fuck are you?'

'Boyle. Colonel Boyle.' He marched up and slammed Lenin's pass onto the table. Krylenko scanned it swiftly, then looked up once again. 'So?' he challenged gruffly.

'What is your rank?' Joe demanded.

'That's none of your business,' Krylenko replied defiantly.

'It is my business. I believe I outrank you.'

'Irrelevant.' He turned his head aside and spat on the floor.

'Stand up, man, when a superior officer is talking to you.'

Krylenko remained firmly seated. 'I have been appointed by the joint leaders of the Revolutionary Government to take charge of the Russian Army here at Stavka Headquarters. I have to answer to no one.'

'But you're not in charge, are you? You cannot control your men.'

'The man was a traitor. He refused to carry out the Government's orders. You cannot blame the men.'

'I am not blaming them. I am blaming you, Krylenko. No one, least of all your commanding officer, should be subjected to the horrific treatment we have just witnessed.'

'It was impossible to stop them. You must have seen that.'

'It was your duty, man. You now say you are their commanding officer. They should surely respect your uniform. Why the hell are you not in uniform anyway?'

'All of this has nothing to do with you. I don't know who you are. And I don't care. Just bugger off - while you can.'

'Are you threatening me?' Joe must have been a terrifying sight as he thundered this challenge, but Krylenko merely waved him away.

But Joe continued, 'I am attached to the British Mission and, for the moment at least, we are Allies. I shall be making a full report on what happened here today.'

If this was intended to unnerve Krylenko, it failed miserably. He held his stance and signalled to a couple of burly men standing by the door who then marched forward and roughly pinned Joe by the arms. He did not resist but spoke again to Krylenko in a more solicitous tone.

'Krylenko. Can I ask you to do one thing at least? Would you please arrange to have the General's body taken to his widow for a decent burial?'

The young man looked up, somewhat incredulous. But then, after a moment's thought, he said simply, 'Agreed.' And then added, 'Now get out.'

Chapter 5

At the Foreign Office, one of the day's principal activities is in progress. Leaning well back in his chair with his eyes to the ceiling, Coldwell's right-hand twiddles a pencil as he ponders seven across of The Times crossword, 'HIJKLMNO'.

'5 letters,' he mutters to himself as he feels the solution to be close by. But a frown of annoyance crosses his brow as the door opens and the dowdy spectacled face of his secretary slowly emerges.

'A Secretary from the Colonial Office is here, Sir. He'd like a word if you could spare a minute.'

'Very well. Show him in.' Tucking the newspaper under a file, he rises to shake hands with his visitor.

'Harry! Haven't seen you for some time,' then adds cheekily, 'don't know whether that's a good thing, or bad.'

Harry smiles, then comes straight to the point, 'Well, old thing, I thought I'd fill you in about this Canadian you've written to me about. Apparently, he was a big player in the Klondike Gold Rush and made a fortune. He seems to want to use the war as his new playground. Anyway, he's a personal friend of the Secretary of State for the Colonies, who wrote a letter of introduction for him. Now, I don't know, he may have used the letter improperly but that's entirely up to you to decide when you reply to your Ambassador. He's not on any Canadian business, I can assure you. It has nothing to do with us.'

This brings a 'tch' from Coldwell, along with a heavy sigh as he realises that the ball has been stuffed firmly back into his court. 'In fact, it gets worse, Harry. We've heard from Buchanan again this morning. The blighter's only on his way down to the Russian Army HQ to talk with the military top brass there. The Russian authorities have been asking Buchanan what he's doing there, and he simply doesn't know how to reply. He doesn't know what the man's up to, I don't know, and nor it seems, do you.'

After a moment's thought, he added, 'We'll have to send it directly to Ottawa - perhaps they'll know. And I'll have to inform the DMI at the War Office. Maybe they can put a tracer on him to curb his activities. Doesn't he realise the damage he could cause? It takes us years of careful diplomacy to gain their confidence and cooperation.'

He pauses briefly, and then, 'Anyway, thanks for the info, Harry. Stay in touch.' They shake hands and Harry leaves him to his more pressing problem - seven across. Sam pokes his head around the door to ask whether he's needed for any follow-up. Coldwell doesn't reply to this, but simply repeats the clue he has been struggling with, 'HIJKLMNO, 5 letters.'

'Water,' says Sam as he leaves, disgruntled.

Coldwell thinks for a couple of seconds, then nods and pencils in the answer.

With Dukhonin's death, Joe's options had suddenly become more limited. George, on the other hand, had quickly identified several potentially useful lines of investigation. The Army was split on the Bolshevik government's decision to call for a ceasefire, with rank-and-file soldiers deserting in droves. London would certainly be very interested in any first-hand information he could gather, and there was no better place for this than Stavka.

But Joe had different priorities. He needed to find out whether provisions were getting through to the battlefields and decided to visit the southwestern front. With the chaos that reigned at Stavka, he was forced to make liberal use of Lenin's pass to get any passage for Carriage 451. He finally succeeded in getting it hitched to an army special carrying a Company of raw recruits, nervously shepherded onboard by their officers who were still loyal. After some four hours, uneventful except for a few lengthy stops, a steady *crump, crump, crump* gave warning that they were approaching hostilities. Austrian forces had advanced toward the town of Tarnopol, and it was here that the relief soldiers disembarked. Joe's carriage was uncoupled and shunted into one of the sheds in the station yard.

Joe found himself at a bit of a loss. With George otherwise occupied, he had hoped to be assigned an interpreter, but none was available when he left Stavka. He might find an officer with a smattering of English, but for the moment at least, they were all too busy organising their troops.

'My name is Stephen Locker, Sir.'

A man in a shabby ill-fitting suit appeared in front of Joe, standing rigidly to attention.

Hugely surprised, Joe played for time.

'At ease, Soldier.' After a couple of seconds, he continued, 'From your manner, I assume you are military.'

'Royal Navy, Sir.'

'I have so many questions, I don't know where to start,' said a puzzled Joe. He finally decided on the one that might provide answers to most of his questions.

'Why are you not in uniform?'

'I'm afraid I lost it, Sir. '

'*You lost it,*' Joe barked. 'How the hell can you lose your uniform?'

Steve hesitated, not sure whether the question was rhetorical. Eventually, he said apologetically, 'I'd rather not say, if you don't mind, Sir.'

Joe heaved a sigh. 'Ah well. So what is your rank?'

'Two and a half rings, Sir. Lieutenant-Commander.'

'Well, let's drop formalities, eh? I'm not even sure I outrank you. And anyway, my rank is Canadian and simply honorary.'

The Brit held out his hand and said, 'Steve', to which Joe responded in kind.

'Right. Next question. What on earth are you doing in this godforsaken town?'

'I'm attached to the British Mission in Mogilev. That's the town that plays host to the Stavka which is always the name given to the current Russian Army HQ. I've got a wide-ranging brief, basically to help out wherever help is needed. At the moment, I'm in command of a small armoured car detachment attempting to save the town from the Austrians. But it's a hopeless task.'

'I'd appreciate it if you'd tell me all about it, Steve. Is there somewhere in town where we can get a drink and something to eat? And a bed would be good.'

'There's very little, I'm afraid. Most of the residents have already left for the country. You could bunk up with me for the night, but it won't be very comfortable.'

'No problem,' said Joe. 'I've got access to my railway carriage. I can sleep there, and I'm sure we can eat there too. My man will complain about the lack of notice, but he should be able to rustle something up.'

Over scrambled eggs and a cup of strong tea, Steve set out the sad state of Tarnopol's defences. 'I don't believe the Austrian army has any idea how little resistance we could put up against a concerted attack. Officers and men who have not deserted are tired and dispirited. Most of our front-line defence relies on a Death Battalion of feisty women set up around the town's borders with orders to shoot anything that moves. Believe me, it's a very dangerous place to be in. And today's trainload was the first we've received in several days. The food and arms supplies are very welcome, of course, but I can't see the new soldiers waiting around long enough to be of any use.'

'What a disaster,' exclaimed Joe. 'I do have a degree of influence in high places. Is there anything I can do to help, do you think?'

Steve shook his head. 'It's all too late now, I'm afraid. Even with a reliable rail system, nothing could get here in time to save the town.'

'Hmm. I'm sure glad I ran into you, Steve,' said Joe, 'I'd have been lost here without you.'

'I believe you'll find that it was I who ran into you. I had a call from Stavka, someone called George - I didn't get his surname. He asked me to keep a lookout for you.'

Joe nodded in appreciation. 'Thank you, George,' he thought.

Steve stayed the night in one of the extra sleeping compartments until they were suddenly awakened by a heavy bombardment of the town. Steve tore out of his bunk without breakfast and returned almost immediately behind the wheel of one of his armoured cars, shouting for Joe to jump in. As he did so, a loud whine announced the arrival of enemy aircraft. Just seconds later, machine gun bullets were thumping into the tarmac of the station yard and, with a crashing of gears and screeching of brakes, Steve raced for cover.

He reached a canopied building and skidded around to watch the action. Three Fokker aircraft were bombing and machine-gunning Joe's train as it lay trapped at the platform. Whether by design or a lucky accident, one bomb hit the tender, blowing it up into the air and way off the rails. It was only then that they realised that many of the new soldiers must have been billeted overnight on the train and were now scattering, fleeing for their lives away from the train.

The three planes banked into tight turns and roared down along the length of the train once again, all the while strafing the helpless running men. A second lucky bomb hit the engine and a fire broke out in one of the coaches. By this time the yard was littered with screaming wounded men, but it was at this moment that Joe's jaw dropped in amazement as an extraordinary scene began to play out.

Into this chaos appeared a white horse, ridden at high speed by a woman, her long blond hair streaming behind her, and powerful legs clad only in blue shorts, ankles digging into the flanks of the bareback horse. At a distance, Joe could not make out her face but his attention was immediately drawn to the incongruous shirt, tie, jacket and cap she was wearing. They were those of a British Royal Navy officer, with two

45

and a half golden rings decorating the arms that held the reins. Even with the tragic scene in front of him, a wide grin spread over Joe's face as he turned to Steve.

'Valkyrie.' His friend announced with a hint of pride.

'You dirty beast. You were screwing her, weren't you? She stole your uniform while you were asleep.'

'Something like that.' He confirmed sheepishly. 'She leads the Death Battalion I told you about. She probably thought it would add some extra level of authority over her girls.

Joe was still smiling as he turned back to watch her weave deftly in and out of buildings, dodging bullets as the Fokkers made one final pass.

And a further surprise was to follow. As she rode out of one of the sheds, she was followed by a couple of British nurses, with their distinctive large red cross on their chests, running towards the casualties scattered around the yard.

This spurred Joe into action. 'Thank the Lord.' He shouted. 'We must set up a medical centre in one of those sheds. Come on...'

Steve needed no second call and sped off towards the nurses. With no time for pleasantries, they pointed to the building from which they had emerged. 'If you've come to help, there are a few beds in there and some tables. We can construct a couple of operating tables - under the lights. And get some help to move these poor devils inside. The planes may be back at any time.'

The two bustled off leaving Joe and Steve wondering what to tackle first. Apart from the wounded, the station yard was now empty save for a couple of miserable-looking Lieutenants, frustrated shepherds who had lost all their sheep. They seemed relieved when Steve, with a combination of gestures and a few Russian words he had picked up that were not bedroom related, asked for their help in getting the casualties indoors.

The next couple of hours would remain in one corner of Joe's memory for the rest of his life. No sooner had the two men completed the nurses' instructions than a constant stream of wounded soldiers were being processed by Julie and Rosemary. Joe could see that Steve was in trouble. Deathly pale and sweating profusely, he was unable to look at many of the gruesome wounds and Joe immediately dispatched him to find more medical supplies.

A number of the casualties were pronounced dead on arrival by the nurses and their bodies were carried out again by the Russian officers. Others were too badly injured to survive, their internal organs damaged beyond repair. These men spent the last few minutes of their lives lying on a bed, their hands held by sweet-smelling angels whispering words of comfort in a tongue they didn't understand.

Cruel injuries to the human body were not unfamiliar to Joe. During the last few years in the Alaskan goldfields, one of his giant dredgers had buckled and collapsed into the icy waters of the Klondike River. Flying chains and shards of twisted metal play terrible havoc with the body's soft tissue, such that human eyes should never have to witness. It was therefore with fearful anticipation that he shouldered the task of assisting the nurses at the operating tables.

The girls had only the basic instruments and medication they held in their cases so their work was extremely rudimentary. The two Russian officers found some fresh sheets and towels and boiled up a plentiful

47

supply of hot water. As the work progressed, Joe's mind began to wander, perhaps in an attempt to blot out the awful sights in front of him, and he began to consider his own plight. He should never have visited the war front and, whatever the outcome, he was certain to be in trouble with his sponsors in London. The town was clearly about to be overrun and they had to get out right now. The train they arrived on was surely unusable, so what were the alternatives? Steve's armoured vehicle would be a good choice for just the two of them but there were many others to consider. And if he were to leave without it, he would permanently lose the use of Carriage 451.

A pile of large boxes came through the open door. As they were deposited on a table, Steve's face appeared from behind them. 'Robbed a pharmacy,' he announced. One of the nurses pounced on them excitedly. 'There's a load of painkillers including some morphine sulphate, some antiseptic bandages, and other sterile stuff, OK?' Rosemary nodded her thanks.

Joe took a moment's leave and took Steve aside. 'Well done, Steve, but we must get out of here - and quick. Could you make sure our carriage hasn't been damaged? It seems to be our best chance of carrying all of us, including the wounded. And we'll need an engine, of course. Scout around. I feel sure a station this size will have something, even if it's just an old shunting engine. It's only got one carriage to pull. And then find a driver. Ask the Station Master. He'll know if there is one. You can offer a driver really good money to take us to Stavka. I know it's quite a way, but it's sure to have a good military hospital.'

'Got it,' said Steve, and added somewhat sarcastically, 'Should be simple enough.'

Joe smiled. 'Off you go then. Oh, and ask how long it will take to get up steam.'

'Yes, Boss.' And within seconds, he was off in his Jeep with a screech of tyres.

The invasion storm continued to rage outside as the grim work continued until the last piece of metal had been teased from the flesh, and a range of patched-up bodies was lined up on beds ready to go. But go where? The Russian officers had bravely held their stations, helping out when needed and comforting their comrades.

And then, during a brief lull in the bombing, all eyes in the room looked up as they heard the *whoop-whoop* of a train whistle, signalling success for Steve. As if by magic, just as the last whistle died away, Steve entered, beaming from ear to ear. Oddly, it was one of the injured Russian soldiers who eased himself up in bed and started the applause.

'It'll be another half hour, folks. They had a couple of engines and, luckily for us, the crew of one had anticipated that one would be needed and lit the boiler three hours ago. It's very nearly up to temperature but still has to be hooked up to 451. Let's get the wounded on board.'

'Have you warned Ivan?' Joe asked.

'Yes,' Steve answered brightly. 'From what you said about him, I thought he might throw a tantrum but he was brilliant. I left him slaving away, making up temporary beds, cutting sandwiches and generally getting the place ready. Come on. Let's go.'

A frenzied thirty minutes later they were all set to go. Rosemary took Joe aside, 'Joe, you were magnificent. Everybody was, of course, but very few people could face the sights you had to cope with. Your help was invaluable.'

'Huh! I was just the oily rag, Rosemary. My admiration for what you two girls achieved knows no bounds and I'll be sure to report it to the Authorities. But that's enough backslapping for now. There's still work to be done.'

'That's what I wanted to talk to you about, Joe. Julie and I have been sent here to help assist with casualties of the battle for Tarnopol, and that's not over yet. Am I to assume we are invited to travel on your train?'

'You certainly are, Rosemary. There are nineteen very sick men on board, many of them critical, and it's going to be at least four or five hours before we can get them to the Stavka hospital. We need you - desperately. Please.'

'I'm not sure, Joe. I really ought to speak with Stavka. We're the last bit of medical help in town.'

'The town's ready to be overrun, Rosemary. Don't worry. The Austrians are sure to have a medical unit. Your job at the moment is to care for these soldiers until they're safe in the hospital. And that's an order, Nurse. OK.'

Rosemary smiled. 'Yes, Sir.' She saluted dramatically, no doubt relieved at not having to take the decision.

As the train chuffed slowly out of the station, Joe began to wonder whether the little shunter engine would be man enough for the job, for the heavily armoured carriage was more than fully laden. Almost all the floor space was taken up by the injured so the poor nurses were forced into highly convoluted movements as they moved between patients.

The train had not travelled more than five miles before a sole Fokker appeared from nowhere and roared over the short train.

Passengers ducked instinctively, expecting the worst, but the pilot was perhaps making a test run and nothing was fired. Anxious eyes shifted to the windows only to see the plane bank sharply to the right and line up for a second pass. Hoping that the smoke might help obscure the target, they held their breath and hoped for the best.

But again, no bombs nor any hail of bullets. The plane lifted steeply into the sky with its wings dipping from side to side in a goodbye salute. Steve turned towards Joe with a look of bewilderment but found him oddly unperturbed, with even the semblance of a smile on his lips. The danger seemingly over, he found his way over to Joe who let him into his little secret.

'I took a little break when you were all busy getting the injured on board. Came across some decorating stuff and painted a large red cross on a white square on the roof of the carriage. There was no red paint and I had to use dark brown. But hey! It worked.'

'Great thinking, Joe.' Steve had passed command of his group to his Russian Sergeant and, with the Austrian army hammering at the gate, had remembered to put his vehicle well out of commission.

'What do you fancy doing now?' Joe asked him.

Steve laughed. 'I'll do whatever they want me to do. I know where I'd like to go - Rumania.'

'Why's that?' asked Joe, surprised. 'I believe I know where it is, but that's about all.'

'They're lovely people, Joe. I have Rumanian relatives and I've often visited them. Now, the country is surrounded by hostile powers and their small army won't be able to hold out for long. It's a poor country and the peasant population is dying of starvation.'

'Who leads the country?'

'It's a monarchy,' pronounced Steve. 'The King is pretty ineffectual though, and it was his English wife that insisted the country sided with the Allies. She's a Granddaughter of Queen Victoria.'

'Sounds like a sorry tale,' said Joe.

'It is,' agreed Steve. 'I'd love to get more help for them.'

'Maybe we'll get a chance. Let's see,' said Joe as he moved to his desk to make a start on the reports he would be making on the action at Tarnopol.

Chapter 6

If Joe's libido had been aroused by the nurses in Tarnopol, as a much younger man newly arriving in Dawson City, it would have been sorely tested. For the waves of masculinity that had invaded the town had attracted a variety of women to meet all their assorted needs. Belle and "Gorgeous" Gussie Lamont were dancers at the Monte Carlo night club and it was here that the two men visited on their first evening in town. They soon learned how expensive it was in Dawson City and realised they would have to get a job - and fast.

Frank was busy at the bar trading drinks for news - of the White Pass trail they've blazed, the American miners' strike, and the Corbett v Fitzsimmons fight. But Joe Boyle's immediate thirst was for knowledge and, with the sky-high prices they had found in town, speed was of the essence. So many questions - who are the major players in town, how is the gold found and extracted, and what was the best way to get concessions? The initial gold strike was nearly a year ago now, so he'd be playing catch up.

Joe spent a while looking around the crowded saloon, his eyes eventually settling on a table in a quiet corner where three oldtimers were chatting and laughing. As he approached, a friendly sweep of an arm invited him to take the fourth chair.

'Welcome, stranger,' greeted a tall, elderly man with thinning hair. 'Are you lost?'

All three laughed out loud. 'Forgive my friend,' said a more portly, ruddy-faced man. 'This place is not much fun, so we tend to josh about quite a bit. You here for the gold?' he teased, and the smiles remained on their faces.

Joe was well used to banter and wasn't to be put off. 'Hi guys,' he started. 'The name's Joe - Joe Boyle. Came in yesterday. You boys miners?' They all nodded their heads, their smiles vanishing.

'Yup,' confirmed Lofty. Whether through height or age, he seemed to be the leader of the group and Joe would concentrate his efforts on him. 'I'm Dave, by the way. Do you have a job?'

'No,' said Joe. 'As I say, we've only just arrived. Are they difficult to come by?'

'Nah. There's loads of work. If it's in Dawson, you should be able to get $10 a day, but out in the mines - maybe $15.'

'I'd better become a miner then. I learn fast.'

'I hear Swifty's looking for more men. What you say, boys. Would Swifty be a good place to start?'

Joe was suspicious. Were they still joshing him - trying to seat him on a bucking bronco?

'I warn you. I'm good with horses.'

Dave laughed briefly but, not getting the reference, 'Swifty ain't a horse. 'Swiftwater' Bill Gates is a miner like us, 'cept he's more successful. He's broken out a bit now though - bought this place, the biggest saloon in town. And he brings in a load of women.' The other two started grinning and cranking their arms in lewd signs.

'I don't think Bill's here tonight,' Tubby cut in.

'Don't worry. It'll be an early night for us tonight,' said Joe. Then, after a short pause, 'So, once I've mastered the job, how do I stake my claim?'

'Afraid you've just about missed the boat there, man. There ain't many stakes left - none in Bonanza and very few in Eldorado. 'Course there's some for sale. Lots of people have left for the Outside, either in disgust or very rich. But beware, Joe. There's loads of corruption about - even in the Mining Recorder's Office. You don't want to pay good money for a worthless stake - and there's loads of them.'

The third man, small and pudgy with a huge drooping black moustache, suddenly woke up. 'But how's he gonna tell a no-good site, Dave? It's a lottery. Remember Andrew Hunker?'

'Yeah,' agreed Tubby. 'And that Swede, what's his name - Anderson? He agreed to buy a "worthless" claim at a drunken party. They laughed at him when he sobered up and tried to withdraw from the deal, but then it turned out to be one of the richest tributaries in the Klondike River. I tell you, you can't never tell.'

'If you ask me,' Dave came in. 'There's more money to be made outside of mining the gold. Swifty had the right idea when he bought this place. Must be making a fortune. Wish I'd thought of it earlier.'

Joe got to his feet. 'Well, it's been nice meeting you, gentlemen. I'm sure we'll see each other around but I'm for bed right now.'

'You in a tent?'

'Yes.'

'Mind your valuable stuff then.'

Joe smiles. 'I don't have much. Good night.'

'You won't want to be living in a tent this winter,' Dave muttered.

This remark stopped Joe in his tracks and he turned to sit down again.

'Tell me about winter, Dave. I guess it's pretty cold, eh.'

The other two laughed, 'You can bet on that, Joe.' Dave agreed. 'In a few weeks, the river will be frozen over 'till March at least. You'll have snow up to your waist, with temperatures down to -25 degrees. We've lost a lot of men living in tents, some from fires or simply freezing to death, hypothermia I think they call it.'

'Why do they stay here in winter? It must be impossible to work.'

This set the three men laughing again. 'Yes,' Dave giggled. 'Yes, it is indeed impossible. But it's also essential. Some of the hardest parts of the work are done in the winter. You've got a lot to learn, boy.'

'Clearly,' Joe grinned as he got up again. 'Thanks for the advice, boys. G'night.'

After the exhausting journey, Joe slept like a log and only awoke with Slavin shaking his shoulder. 'Wake up, Joe. A lot to do.'

As they dunked their dry bread into a tin mug of coffee, Joe told Slavin what he had learned last night. 'We've got to build something to live in, Frank - and fast, 'cos the winter's not far off.'

The two men began a thorough tour of Dawson. Noting the sad line of prospectors besieging the Claims Registration Office, the shops and even many saloons were already open along the muddy main street. Joe stopped outside a builder's store. 'I want to build a log cabin for us, Frank. We've got a few tools, but we'll need more - saws to fell trees and cut the logs, some draw knives to debark them and so on. Let's see what they've got.'

Their meagre bankroll wouldn't go far, and they still had to eat, so Joe asked for some credit. The storeman gave a short laugh, but then asked, 'You got a job?'

'No. We've only just arrived. I intend to get one tonight though. I'm seeing Bill Gates.'

'You a friend of Swifty then?'

'I intend to be - after tonight.'

After a long pause for thought, 'You look a respectable sort. I'll give you a $50 tab for one week. Don't you prove me wrong now?'

'Don't worry. I won't.' Joe assured him. He had never welched on a deal before and didn't intend to start now.

'You won't if you value your skin,' threatened the store owner.

Joe smiled and thanked him. 'I assume I can just build where I like, but where would you say is a good spot.'

'Where the trees are. On the hillside, back of town. You'll see a number being built.'

They left the store each holding an armful of tools and, with no time to delay, spent the rest of the day sorting a site and cutting timber. Slavin was not entirely sold on the idea of prospecting for gold and had already arranged a job, so that evening Joe walked alone down to the Monte Carlo saloon. It was not just a bar, but also a mini night club complete with a dance floor, gambling tables and even a small stage beside which a honky-tonk player was bashing out a background of popular music.

Surrounding the central area was a first-floor gallery with doors to rooms that suggested all manner of exciting activities. As Joe entered, he was jostled by a throng of miners bent on spending their hard-earned gold dust like the water from whence it had come. Women of all ages, shapes and sizes mingled with them offering a good time to anyone with a small nugget. Joe forced his way through to the crowded bar and ordered sarsaparilla to some odd looks from his neighbours. 'You feeling OK, man?' one of them asked amid chuckling from his pals.

'Why? You offering to buy me a whiskey?' Joe challenged.

'Yeah. Go on, Tommy. Buy the man a real drink. 'E clearly can't afford one.'

Tommy looked sheepish. 'Nah. Think I'll keep my dust.'

Joe smiled as he walked away to join a table with a couple of spare seats. They proved to be good company but he was committed to a loan and, whilst it paled into insignificance beside the massive loans he would eventually arrange, it still needed repayment within a week. He had come here this evening to get a job and needed to speak with "Swiftwater" Bill Gates.

On impulse, he decided to publicly announce his presence in Dawson. The pianist had stopped for a break and Joe excused himself, walked over to the piano and sat down. Nothing changed and the noisy babble continued unabated. Then, with a dramatic flourish, Joe caressed the keys in a cascade of sweeping scales. Heads began to turn as he entered into a medley of popular songs - The Sidewalks of New York, Polly Wally Doodle, Oh Mister Porter, and others. After about ten minutes and another flourish of the keys, he began to sing The Mountains of Mourne.

Rapturous applause greeted the final words, but calls for more were ignored by Joe who knew the wisdom of "always leave them wanting more". On other evenings, there would no doubt be more, but tonight he had other business to attend to.

A short man with a moon face and a straggly black moustache approached Joe with, 'Captain?'

Joe was slightly wrong-footed. 'Swiftwater?' he countered. Bill Gates smiled and offered his hand, which Joe accepted with his renowned firm handshake. He took in, with no outward sign of amusement, the weird dress of the little man - a starched white shirt and short fat tie beneath a brilliant multicoloured waistcoat. Joe himself was known for his dress style, but this was something else. He later learned that Swifty possessed the only starched shirts in Dawson and would never be seen not wearing one - even, it was said, in bed.

'Captain eh? Where did you get that?' Joe asked.

'Ah!' said Bill. 'News of your exploits in Skagway precede you, Sir.'

'Can I buy you a drink?' offered Joe.

'You insult me, Sir. This is my place. I buy drinks for my friends here.' After a short break, he added, 'And a little bird tells me your cash flow isn't exactly up to snuff. Let's talk, Joe.'

He led him to a private booth at the back of the room where a waiter appeared immediately. 'Now, I have some excellent imported whiskey,' Bill declared. 'Can I tempt you, Sir?' Swiftwater had taken on board Joe's nickname and would call him 'Sir' for much of the time.

'I don't normally drink alcohol, Bill, but I don't want to insult you again. I'll have just one - to keep you company.'

'You're after a job, I hear?'

'If you have one.'

'From all reports, you would make a good bouncer for this place. It does get a bit rowdy at times.'

'Maybe later, Bill. For now, I want to learn all about placer gold mining.'

'Yeah, well, I've got a part-claim up in No.13 Eldorado. We're getting a reasonable amount of gold from it. I'd be paying $15 a day. But it's hard work, Joe. Are you sure you're up for it?'

Joe smiled. 'I believe I can manage it. Tell me about the work.'

Swiftwater explained the fundamentals of placer mining - digging shafts and tunnels through the permafrost muck to expose the gravel, which had then to be extracted and sifted for gold. It certainly sounded like hard and dull work and, even as it was being described, Joe experienced doubts about its efficiency. 'There are other methods, of course. You could simply just panhandle for dust and small nuggets that had been washed down into the many streams and creeks, but the pickings are generally small and elusive.'

They talked of many things that first evening. Bill was generous in passing on his knowledge and experience, and Joe lapped it all up with avarice. There was laughter too, and gradually a close bond between the two began to form.

They met again the following morning when Bill took Joe up to the Eldorado site, introduced him to his fellow miners, showed him around the current workings and set him a couple of testing tasks which he passed with ease.

Joe and Frank had very little time to spend in the many saloons of Dawson. When not working, they were building their log cabin. For relaxation, Joe walked far and wide plotting a new personal vision of the future of gold mining in the area. The Klondyke River is fed by numerous tributaries whose beds and shores were shown to be rich in gold. Rather than laborious placer mining and panhandling, he would introduce industrial-scale methods. In his mind's eye, he could see huge dredgers, operating round the clock to haul out and sieve the gold-bearing gravel in their giant buckets. Lines of communication between the Yukon and the rest of the world were fragile in the extreme, and every section of these massive machines would need to be carried over the existing difficult passes and be assembled on site. This would require a raft of new supporting services, including better transportation, workshops and electric power plants. The risks involved in such a huge investment would demand watertight concessions on large tracts of land and river, such that had never been granted before.

Neither Dawson's Registration office nor the local Gold Commissioner had sufficient authority for this size of claim and Joe was referred to Clifford Sifton, the new Interior Minister in Ottawa which meant another hazardous journey to the "Outside".

Joe broke the news of his plans to Slavin, 'I've prepared this application for about 8 miles frontage of the Klondike river, Frank. I've signed it and it's all ready to be lodged at the Registration Office. It probably won't be considered locally, but I have to start somewhere and it's what I'll be pressing for in Ottawa. Sign it, Frank, and get the process started.'

In the Eldorado workings, Joe laid it out to Swifty. 'We've talked about it before, Bill. You know I'm not convinced by this method of gold mining. You'll never recover more than a quarter of the gold, and I want much more. I intend to use large hydraulic dredgers costing huge amounts of capital, and that will no doubt require sizeable concessions. I won't be able to get them locally, so I'm off to Ottawa in a couple of days.'

'You've left it a bit late, Joe. The big freeze is only a short way off.'

'That's why I'm leaving as soon as possible. But I've got a few things to do first - getting the boat ready for one thing.'

Later that day Bill sought Joe out. 'I've been thinking, Joe,' he started. 'I need some new blood in the saloon. I gotta compete with other bars in town, and they've got a whole new bunch of girls.'

After a short pause, 'So, how do you feel about me coming with you, Captain.'

'Glad to have you aboard, Bill.'

They shook hands and then gave each other a hug.

Chapter 7

Both Boyle's recent actions and his reports on the railways had begun to attract the favourable attention of the Russian authorities. But in London, it is almost too much to bear for the Foreign Office. Following some press stories, Coldwell is hauled upstairs to a meeting with the Foreign Minister himself. 'Can you explain why this middle-aged civilian foreigner is engaged in active service under the auspices of the British Mission? What's he doing there?'

'He's been a mystery throughout, Sir. The Canadians disown him. So does the War Office. It's only the Russians that seem to find him useful.'

'Well, we've made some strange bedfellows in this conflict. If he is of help to the Russian war effort, then he's our friend too.' He pauses for thought. 'What damage can he do?'

Coldwell did not reply immediately, and the Foreign Minister continued, 'Do you consider him some sort of security risk?'

Coldwell squirms, 'No. Not really. But he could undermine some of the relationships we have striven for years to foster. Reports suggest he may be moving on to Rumania now. God knows what he'll be getting up to there.'

'From what I've heard, he's been sorting out the Russian railway system with some success. And God knows, those poor Rumanians need all the help they can get. If the Russians are comfortable with what he's up to, I don't see why we should interfere. Let's cut him some slack, eh? Keep a watching brief, but give him his head.'

The unannounced arrival of the train back at Stavka must have raised both concern and a degree of amusement at the sight of the tiny toy engine pulling Joe's oversize coach. But it was not long before a fleet of ambulances was ferrying the wounded soldiers to the Army Hospital. Word soon got around and the heroic work of all involved was celebrated. The following day, in front of the morning parade, Joe was decorated with the Order of Stanislav.

He had been surprised not to see George in the welcoming crowds, but soon learned that he had been granted an interview with the newly appointed Prime Minister, Alexander Kerensky. He had left early that morning and was not expected back for three or four days. Joe spent the day writing a variety of reports on the events in Tarnopol and letters of commendation for the brilliant work by Steve, the two English nurses, the Russian officers, and the crew of the getaway train. Even Steve's Valkyrie got a mention. As he wrote her name, he wondered what had befallen her and throughout his life, an image of the brave lady sidled into his mind from time to time.

In the evening, he met up with Steve who continued to lobby for the Rumanian cause. Joe had been moved by their plight and eventually agreed to a visit provided it could be combined with some investigation into the reputedly poor rail system through Bessarabia to Bucharest. 451 would have to be left behind for some repairs, but Joe managed to secure an ordinary compartment on the following day's train.

It proved to be a languorous all-stations stopping train except that, in practice, it made very few stops. Joe sought out the guard, who explained that stopping was prohibited at unstaffed stations, of which there were many for the same sort of reasons as he had heard in Moscow. This resulted in additional delays as the train's staff were regularly forced to switch necessary points and signals.

At one point, the train screeched to a halt, just inches before ploughing into a long convoy of fully loaded freight wagons. There was found to be no engine at either end and the signals were set against it, suggesting to the guard that it was most likely an act of sabotage. With no time to investigate further, the wagons were laboriously shunted into a siding at the next station, and the train was on its way.

To preserve the ancient fabric of the Rumanian capital, the King had been persuaded to declare Bucharest an open city. The overpowering Austro-German forces commanded by Field Marshal von Mackensen had cut through the feeble Rumanian army like a knife through butter, and now surrounded much of the city. The train came to a stop in a station seething with an anxious population trying to leave the city, and Joe wondered whether it would be wise to follow suit. Stepping out onto the platform, Steve turned to him and urged him to follow. 'It's an open city. You'll be quite safe,' he promised.

Somewhat reluctantly, Joe followed him off the train and they were able to book into the Manuc's Inn hotel where they met up with Colonel Chris Thompson, one of the few remaining members of the British Mission in Bucharest. Over dinner, they recounted their recent exploits in Tarnopol and in return the Colonel brought them up to date with a very similar position in Bucharest. Although already pronounced an open city, occupying forces would not be present in any numbers until after the next day's ceremonial victory parade.

Field Marshal August von Mackensen cut a most ferocious figure. Sitting astride a white charger, he led the noon parade as it marched through the streets of Bucharest wearing full Hussar dress, including the fearsome "Totenkopf" busby with its death's head emblem. The parade was watched by a few glum residents, but not by Joe Boyle. He had been roused very early by a series of loud thumps on his door. Rubbing the sleep out of his eyes, he opened them to reveal a much too lively Steve.

'Wakey wakey. The hotel wants us out. Get dressed, collect all your kit together and get down to reception. We've got to check out and be gone in the next twenty minutes. We've got another job to do.'

'Another job?' Joe instantly recalled the criticism caused by his visit to the front line at Tarnopol. 'What sort of job?'

'Oh, just a bit of demolition. We have to blow up a couple of oil wells.' With that, he turned and left with, 'See you downstairs.'

Many of the Balkan states are blessed with considerable reserves of oil, and Rumania has its fair share. To the south and west of Bucharest, the Walachian fields had largely been destroyed to deny them to the approaching enemy forces, but Chris Thompson had received an intelligence report that a couple of the more important wells were still in commission. As an engineer, he had some knowledge of explosives, but he brought with him a real demolition expert in the stout form of Sergeant Sam Fuller. A big man in every dimension, he took up considerably more than his fair share of space in the Austin armoured car that sped along deserted roads. Shackled behind it was a small trailer full of explosives which should have limited the speed to 20 mph, but Steve thought only of the urgency of their mission.

The party was relieved to find no one at the first well. Parking several hundred yards short of it, Joe and Steve helped to carry the heavy boxes of dynamite to the rig and were then summarily dismissed back to the car. There, they had an anxious wait for almost half an hour until, without any notice, an enormous explosion was immediately followed by a blast of hot air. It was all very dramatic and they both leapt out of the car to get a better look at the spectacle. Sadly, although there was certainly a large amount of fire and smoke, there was nothing of the huge plumes of oil on fire they expected. Had the charge failed?

It was another twenty minutes before Sam and Chris came jogging into view. They immediately pronounced success and urged a speedy departure. Steve needed no encouragement and was through the gears in no time. Asked about the lack of burning oil, Sam explained that, although the oil did frequently ignite, the function of the blast was simply to warp and rip open the steel casing of the drill to allow in sand and water, and hopefully also to crack and twist the pipe itself.

'That's why we were so long getting back to you. We had to make sure the rig was both unusable and irreparable.'

'Well done you two,' exclaimed Joe. 'One more, eh.'

Well 45 was close by and looked to be more important, being set within several substantial buildings, all now seemingly unoccupied. Apart from these, the whole area appeared to be deserted with mile after mile of uncultivated rough ground. Steve parked the car a little nearer this time and in full view of the rig, but he and Joe were again forcefully sent back once the explosives had been delivered to the site. They watched for a while as the two distant figures flitted around the wellhead packing in the sticks of dynamite and running fuses.

But Joe was beginning to feel unsettled. Whilst aware of the importance of their current task, it was far removed from his own mission's terms of reference. It was not difficult to console himself that all his activities contributed to the war effort, but they were also delaying his final report on the railway system. Knowing that they would have a wait of at least half an hour, he reached into his briefcase for a notebook and began to write up the current events.

An hour had passed without any explosion when Steve spotted the Colonel approaching swiftly and looking grim as he reached the car.

'As you've probably guessed, we hit some problems. I won't go into details now but...' His words faded out as his eyes followed Steve's finger pointing to the distant horizon with shouts of, 'Looks like the enemy's arriving...'

The Colonel swung his binoculars from around his body and clamped them to his eyes. 'He's right,' he shouted. 'On horseback, and they're heading straight for us.'

"Crack! Boom!" The explosion drowned his last words, and a few seconds later the long-awaited column of flaming oil shot high into the air.

'Bravo, Sam,' shouted the Colonel.

'Yes. Great work indeed, Sam,' Joe agreed enthusiastically. 'But, Chris, there's no way we can reach him before the cavalry arrives.'

The Colonel paused only briefly before he accepted. 'No. They'll be on us within minutes.'

As Steve started up the engine, Joe leapt out of the car and went around to the back. Valuable seconds passed with Steve pumping excitedly at the accelerator.

'What the fuck's he doing?' he screamed, but still no Joe.

They could hear the sound of galloping hoofs before the door swung open and Joe dived in shouting 'Go, Go, Go.'

He hadn't finished the last 'Go', nor closed the door before the car leapt wildly and surged forward as fast as the gears would allow. As the first *ping* told them that the cavalry had arrived within firing range, the Colonel shouted 'It's the Austrian light cavalry.'

'I don't give a fuck who they are,' screamed Steve. 'They're firing at us. What the hell were you doing out there, Joe? Having a pee before we leave?'

As more lead attempted to pierce the armour plating, in their frenzied imagination they could hear the horses' hoofs galloping alongside, but in truth the noise of the over-revving engine made any other sound impossible to hear.

'I'll tell you later,' shouted Joe.

Inside the car, the three men hunched anxiously wondering how well the armour would protect them from the onslaught. Outside, the pursuing cavalrymen were having their own difficulties. With their useless sabres hanging from their waists, firing their carbines with any accuracy from the back of their speeding steeds was difficult enough, but reloading them was completely impossible. And the few bullets that did hit their target appeared to be deflected harmlessly away.

The frantic duel seemed to continue forever, but in fact, it lasted for only a few minutes. Inevitably, the pursuers could not maintain the necessary speed and dropped away one by one. When Steve saw the last horse pull up, its rider gloomily watching the car disappear into the distance, he let out a loud cheer and throttled down the speed. The other two joined in celebrating their survival with whoops of relief.

When the merriment died away, the Colonel suddenly became serious and exclaimed, 'I am so sorry we couldn't save Sam.'

'Don't go blaming yourself,' Joe said. 'He's unarmed and will certainly surrender himself. The Austrian Cavalrymen are honourable and will treat him well, for sure.' After a short pause, he continued, 'He'll be held as a prisoner of war for the duration - bed and all meals found...'

Joe's mild attempt at humour failed to amuse the Colonel, but he did not raise the issue again. To ease the silence, Steve quickly changed the subject, 'So, Joe. Why did you leave the car at such a critical time?'

'To save our lives,' Joe stated enigmatically.

He milked the silence of his companions, until Steve asked, 'How so?'

'I'd spent long enough on the journey sitting in front of a timebomb, so I got out to uncouple the trailer. Don't forget, there were still a couple of boxes of dynamite left in it and I didn't want enemy fire to set it off right behind my back.'

'Of course,' mused Steve. 'Neither of us thought of that.'

'I guessed we might have to make a quick getaway, so I practised detaching it while we waited for Sam and Chris to blow up the first well.'

'Thanks, Joe. You're forgiven.'

The Colonel had been studying the crude map we had been provided with and suddenly piped up, 'I'm not quite sure where we are - or where we're going. Can we have a conflab?'

It was Steve who came up with the semblance of a plan.

'We can't go back to Bucharest - that's for sure. It'll certainly be firmly in enemy hands by now. I take it we need to find a rail connection back to Stavka and I think the best bet is to aim for Jassy. It's the new centre of government with the Royal Family already relocated there. It's right up in the northeast corner of the country, so it'll be quite a long journey.'

'How are we doing for fuel? Are we going to have enough?'

'The short answer is, no. We've got a couple of cans, but she's a thirsty beast and we'll have to find a lot more. We'll be in friendly territory all the way and there are bound to be some towns. And we'd better find a better map.'

'All agreed then? That's east until we're past Bucharest, and then north.'

They all nodded, grunting their agreement, and settled down for the long journey as comfortably as the sparse comforts of the cabin would allow.

Everyone they came across was warm and friendly. Many of them were clearly in trouble, with whole families close to starvation. A farm they called in was typical, but the farmer and his wife insisted that the three of them sit down for something to eat. A few vegetables boiled into a thin soup and a crust of stale bread were difficult to force down, but they realised that this was probably the peasants' only fare - set to last them for several days. Thankfully, they were allowed to spend the night on straw in one of the deserted stables, covered by a variety of motley blankets and other bed coverings.

As they prepared to leave, the farmer asked in passable German if they were alright for fuel. Chris understood and jumped on this promising remark. 'Why? Do you have any to spare?'

'I do. I keep a good supply for my tractor, but I won't be using it much until the Spring.'

'We'll take all you can spare,' Chris said excitedly.

The farmer took Steve into one of the sheds and emerged with four large cans.

Joe, who always made sure he had a good supply of local currency, got out a roll of lei. When the farmer noticed this, he held up his hand and shook his head. He told Chris that we were on an important mission to assist his country. We were allies and he would take no money. Using hand signals, Joe asked, 'For your wife perhaps, who fed us last night?'

He was adamant. 'Nu,' he insisted.

Joe stood for a while, nonplussed, then thrust the bundle of notes back into his pocket. He realised it would be useless, perhaps rude even, to insist any further. But as they left, he detached a gold badge from one of the lapels of his uniform and gently pinned it to the front of his wife's dress. The farmer looked on, smiling his thanks. Joe knew that both were unaware that it was crafted from pure Yukon gold. She would probably wear it until her dying day and they would never benefit from its considerable value.

Hours later, fuel was again causing concern. Their spirits were lifted by the sight of civilization appearing on the horizon, although they realised it wasn't Jassy which was still another couple of hours away. It turned out to be only a small village, but it was playing host to a sizable military hospital. Originally a complex of agricultural buildings, it was one of many that had been hastily constructed as the war casualties mounted.

Steve and Chris went off to find some fuel and perhaps to cadge a meal, leaving Joe to stretch his aching legs. With no apparent security, he was able to wander into a large hanger barn. Climbing a few steps onto a crude gallery, he was stunned by the scene that met his eyes. Three long rows of beds were occupied by soldiers with every conceivable type of battle wound. A few were propped up on pillows, but most were comatose, swaddled in bandages and attached to a variety of tubes running in life-giving fluids. In the corridors between them, dozens of nurses flitted between beds, assisting doctors and attending patients with all manner of clinical equipment. Joe stood mesmerised, wondering how order could be derived from such apparent chaos.

He had been watching for a while when his eyes settled on one particular nurse. Taller than most, she moved gracefully between beds, sitting to talk to each broken soldier. Often, she would lean right over his body to whisper words of comfort into his ear, frequently kissing his cheek gently as she rose and started for the next bed. As she glided elegantly from bed to bed, her fellow nurses bustled around her, smiling and chattering, but there was always one of them at the foot of the next bed to brief her on the patient's condition.

Joe watched her for several minutes, transfixed. After a while, unannounced and uninvited, he experienced that old feeling of arousal, a fluttering from somewhere deep within his body. It was odd and took him by surprise, for it had happened once before in recent days, but under very different circumstances. Rosemary, one of the heroic nurses of Tarnopol, was young, pretty and vivacious. But he knew absolutely nothing of this distant vision that had attracted his attention. Both her personality and looks were strangers to him, so why should she spark such a feeling? The answer came to him quickly enough. There was something majestic about the way she moved about exercising her vocation, her selfless efforts to ease the suffering of others.

'So this is where you've been hiding?' Steve suddenly broke the spell. 'We've found some fuel, and I've got some food for you.'

Steve didn't answer immediately, prompting Steve to enquire, 'Are you alright, Joe?'

He didn't wait for a reply but continued, 'Wow. What an amazing sight.' His eyes swept the entire scene from side to side and added sadly, 'All those injured men, their lives changed forever.'

'Yes,' agreed Joe flatly, but then. 'Let's go, Steve.'

The doughty Austin had served them well and the trio spent the final leg of their journey with a sense of relief. This lighter mood was challenged from time to time by examples of the poverty and starvation that pervaded the country. Malnourished children kicking around an old deflated football with legs resembling sticks. A wizened old man sitting at the roadside patting the back of his dog which was nothing more than a small pile of skin and bone, almost certainly already dead.

'I have to thank you, Steve. You have opened my eyes to the terrible suffering of the people of this land, and I join your determination to help them in some way.'

Nothing further was said until they entered the outskirts of Jassy.

'I might stay here for a few days,' Joe said.

'To do what, Joe? You can't stop the Austrian army single-handedly. What do you expect to achieve?'

'I don't know, Steve. I'll ask what help they need. I'll see the Prime Minister. Or King Ferdinand. Or perhaps his English wife…'

'Not easy to get an audience with the Royals," Steve mused.

'Well, you've already seen one of them today,' Chris entered the conversation.

Seconds passed as Joe and Steve looked at one another blankly.

'What on earth do you mean?' Joe asked.

'The Queen. Queen Marie. She was at the hospital. Every morning she visits one or other of the military hospitals, dressed in a fresh white uniform. She is a trained nurse, but spends most of her days providing one-to-one comfort to the wounded soldiers.'

Joe said nothing. He knew immediately that it was Queen Marie that had so impressed him. He recalled thinking that the lady possessed a regal aura, so the revelation came as no great surprise. It did, however, reinforce a steely resolve that sometime, somewhere, he would somehow try to meet up with her.

Chapter 8

It was early morning on a cold October day. Three men dragged their boat down to the edge of the Yukon River.

'We'll be taking the Dalton Trail, Frank,' Joe told Slavin. 'I want to pick up a steamer at Haines Mission in a few days and I'll let you know when I'm settled in Ottawa.'

Travelling upstream was hard work, poling for the most part, but it would only be for two or three days as they planned to ditch the boat at Carmack's Post and leg it down to Haines.

But it would not work out that way. The weather suddenly took a violent change for the worse and temperatures plunged to some 20 degrees below zero. Pack ice quickly began to form in stretches of still water and the collapsible boat collapsed. During the necessary repair work, Swiftwater overreached and fell into the water and under the ice. Joe was swift to act, smashing the ice with an oar and pulling Swifty out by the legs. But he will never forget the look of terror on his friend's face as he looked up through the ice, his eyes pleading for help.

Joe stripped off Swifty's soaking skins and raided his bed roll to envelop him in blankets. But before changing into dry clothes himself, he waded again into the river to retrieve all their gear, for he realised that they would have to abandon the boat and continue on foot. This was hard going in the ever-deepening snow, and it was dusk before lights in the building told them that they would not have the place to themselves. Indeed, it was crowded. As he entered, Joe spotted a group of US mailmen lounging on sacks of undelivered mail.

'I guess the mail's gonna be late again.' Joe's opening attempt at humour was not appreciated, the commodity having been blunted by the blizzard raging outside. For a sizable group of hard men to be confined together for a protracted period in such a small space is not a good idea. Arguments and even fights broke out daily. Joe attempted to ease the tension with stories, songs and jokes but, as the snowstorms continued, his repertoire was soon exhausted.

A young writer, introducing himself as Jack London, tried to fill the void by reading his novels. Joe was impressed, saying, 'I've never been a great reader of fiction, Jack.'

'Well, you should start, Joe. You're sure to be in one of my books someday.' In the event, it was probably later, when Joe had assembled a crack team of huskies, that its imperious leader would become immortalised as White Fang.

A few days later, Joe announced that he and Bill would be making a run for it. 'This shelter was not designed for so many,' he opened. 'Food is already running out and we don't have much fuel. This weather could last all winter and we'll all perish. Each of you has to make up his mind whether he's going to join us. It's not an easy decision. I don't have to paint you a picture of what travel is like in these conditions. It's a well-worn trail and in summer would take about four days but in this… you can triple that at least.'

Only a couple decided to take their chances and stay put, with the remainder happy to leave Joe as Captain to lead the party down to Hains. The rest of the day was spent butchering two horses that had been suffering in a cold outside stable. They were cooked and prepared for the journey which set off in the morning. Travelling in freezing conditions in snowshoes, with no tent or stove, they can only trudge for a few miles each day before finding a thicket of trees or a cliff - somewhere to shelter and try to get some sleep, huddled together.

As the weather worsened, travel became almost impossible and the core strength was gradually sapped from every man. At one point, Joe was forced to make several trips across a river, wading waist-deep, carrying exhausted men together with their packs. Swiftwater, in particular, began to suffer terribly, his slight frame offering little resistance against the persistent strong headwinds. He had reached the point where he would prefer to lie down in the snow and die rather than take another step, with others following suit. Joe would have none of this, of course, and moved amongst them all, encouraging those who would respond to exhortation and praise, whilst spurring others on with swearing and insults.

Eventually, on 23rd November, the party staggered into the small settlement of Haines Mission, each of them realising what a close call it had been. It had taken them a full 25 days but they were thankfully able to get an early passage on a steamship to Seattle.

The Dawson Daily News pronounced the group as being unanimous in their praise of Boyle's leadership, reporting that, 'Every man of the party declares till today that, but for his able management, not one man would have reached the coast alive.'

This was underlined in a dinner at Seattle's Tortoni Hotel when they presented their Captain with a handsome gold watch set with a large diamond and inscribed, 'Presented to Mr J.W.Boyle in token of the expedition from Dawson City to Chilkat, Alaska in token of their appreciation of his most excellent management thereof.'

Swiftwater left for San Francisco, whilst Joe first called at the family home in Woodstock. All of his relationships were destined to suffer on the altar of his wanderlust and the two young children from his first marriage were being brought up by his parents. They ran screaming, "Daddy" the moment he came into sight and he effortlessly scooped up one on each arm and moved towards his smiling parents.

He spent a happy and restful couple of days with the family. After the usual chit-chat of re-entry, his father demanded, 'Well boy, you come back loaded with gold for me?'

Joe smiled. 'Not yet, Pa. But I've got loads of ideas on how it can be done.'

'Hmm. Expensive ones, I'll bet.'

'You're right, Pa. Investments will be huge. You game?'

After a short laugh. 'Huh. I don't have that sort of money, boy. What about your New York company? Your brother says it's going well.'

'I'm talking hundreds of thousands, Pa - maybe millions.

'Any ideas where you can go for funding like that?'

'Not really - no,' Joe admitted. He paused for a while, gathering his thoughts. 'Even before I begin, I'll need firm commitments on some very good mining concessions. I'm talking about miles of frontages to rivers and creeks where I can drag out the gold with giant dredgers, a power station for electricity to drive them, and licences to cut timber. No investor will touch it without such assets. The capital cost for machinery, ships and transportation - it'll be enormous.'

'You make me tired, son. But good luck with it all.'

'I'm told the man to see is the new Interior Minister, Sir Clifford Sifton.'You don't know him, I suppose?'

'Never met him - no,' and then added, 'But I know Harold McGiverin does. I'll have a word with him.'

This chance conversation unlocked a giant door for Joe. He had only just settled into Ottawa's Russell Hotel when he was handed a message offering him a meeting with Sifton. The two men got on famously from the start and found considerable symmetry in their individual ambitions. For some time, Sifton had been pushing for a major development of the region whilst Joe would need a mining concession like no other.

The shape of this concession soon emerged. Much the same as that which Slavin had already lodged in Dawson, it proposed a hydraulic mining claim on both sides of a nine-mile stretch of the Klondike River, starting at Bonanza Creek and extending to the mouth of Hunker Creek. Although the claim was of a totally new scale, Sifton was not phased and gave Joe the green light, indicating that formal consent would soon be granted.

A very happy Joe returned to the Russell Hotel where he settled down to await formal approval. Weeks passed and, with no consent forthcoming, Joe spent his time refining his master plan and talking with other residents, one of whom had entered his unlikely name into the hotel register as Arthur Newton Christian Treadgold. He was later to become one of Joe's greatest competitors and a formidable adversary.

Far from being born to walk on the precious metal as his name suggested, Treadgold was born in Lincolnshire, England. A direct descendant of Sir Isaac Newton, he was highly intelligent and was most tenacious in pursuit of his goals. His persuasive manner deceived Joe for a while and they met frequently, talking late into the night about their mutual interests in music, gold and the Klondike, although Treadgold had never been within 1,000 miles of the area. When he did finally decide to make the journey, Joe trusted him sufficiently to suggest that he examine and report on his proposed concession, a task that allowed the loathsome man to tuck away every little piece of information to use in working up his own rival plan.

Eventually, at the end of June 1898, following a sharp letter from Joe, Sifton renewed support for Joe's proposals, adding timber rights throughout the agreed area. This was the legendary "Boyle Concession" which then caused much consternation in the goldfields. Joe was familiar with controversy but was also aware that nothing worth doing could be achieved without causing it. Change was frequently unwelcome but it went with the territory, and like all other problems had to be properly managed.

On his return, he found Skagway transformed into a boom town although still consumed in lawlessness. "Soapy" Smith had been elected Mayor and ruled the town with his hoodlums, robbing travellers and slitting their throats if they resisted. Those who weren't robbed were fleeced at the gambling tables or by prostitutes.

In Dawson, he finds that a gang of men has entered onto Joe's concession and were harvesting timber, refusing to stop when served notice. In many ways, timber was as important to Joe as the gold, who already had advanced plans for a sawmill. When all efforts to stop the poaching failed, Joe realised that he must take firm action to stop it. He recruited an armed gang of his own to evict anyone without written permission from Government Officials. When this too failed, he began to suspect some illicit dealing and threatened to hold these officials personally responsible for any damage or loss. This exposed the palm-greasing, and the Commissioner was soon removed from his post.

Frank Slavin remained steadfastly averse to picking up a shovel, preferring to act as a guard on bullion trails and whatever he could earn from boxing. Eventually, their partnership ended with Boyle buying his share of the claims for $20,000.

Having secured a good income from the timber, he can acquire a local status symbol - a pack of husky dogs second to none. Composed of MacKenzie River and Malamute huskies, it is headed by their wise leader, Cronja, who is part Timber Wolf. When he decides to escape the previous winter's shortages of food and medicines, Joe is challenged to a contest that he finds impossible to refuse. With such a dog team, he is not daunted by the prospect of a two-month, five-hundred-mile mush to Skagway.

Once again, "Swiftwater" Bill Gates would accompany him and as they swung out of Dawson they met with the opposition for the first time. Although led by an experienced musher, it comprised four miners, all travelling 3rd class, which entailed walking beside the sledge carrying their own kit. Upgrading to 2nd class, their kit could be stowed on the sledge, whilst 1st class would allow them to travel on the sledge themselves. This shabby mob were soon left far in Joe's wake and he set himself a new target of beating the record for the mush to Skagway.

Early snow left them travelling through a virgin white wilderness, but during the fifth week, any chance of a record suddenly vanished as a series of blizzards prevented any possibility of progress. When at last it began to clear, they set off once more following a mountain stream. All of a sudden, "Swiftwater" let out a frightened scream and disappeared from view. Looking back, Joe spotted him clinging to a rock in the middle of a raging torrent of foaming water. With steam billowing over the water, Joe realised that hot thermal springs had melted the underside of a snowy overhang and that his friend had simply crashed through it.

Joe wasted no time and quickly formed a lifeline from the sledge lashings and threw it to "Swiftwater." But he remained clinging to his rock, clearly paralysed with fear. Joe stripped off all his clothes, grabbed the line and leapt into freezing water with a single loud bellow. With Bill still refusing to let go, Joe realised that the fast-flowing water would take him swiftly downstream and into a hole through which the stream disappeared underground. With rapidly numbing fingers, he managed to tie the line around Bill's waist, whereupon he let go of the rock with a shriek of terror. It was only Joe's extraordinary strength that allowed him to drag Bill's body against the flow as it raced towards to hole, and to land him safely on the bank. Together, they lay recovering for several minutes in the freezing snow before donning fresh skins.

When they finally reached Skagway, they were treated royally as Yukon celebrities and on the SS Excelsior "Swiftwater" embellished each new telling of the tale of his ducking.

Christmas was approaching and young Flora Boyle was playing in the front garden of the family home in Woodstock when she spotted two heavily bearded fur-clad men approaching the house. Squinting her eyes, she suddenly recognised Joe and rushed to his outspread arms shrieking "Daddy".

With family greetings over, Joe took Flora to the railway station and introduced her to the dogs. He then decided to give the town a treat. Hitching up the team to their sled, he piled on all their luggage and then seated Flora on top. Like some little queen, she was driven through the centre of town with Joe urging on the dogs, cracking his whip and singing out a variety of mushers' trail commands. It was a happy homecoming.

But it wasn't until late June of the following year the legendary "Boyle Concession" was formally granted and Joe's path forward became clear.

Chapter 9

On arrival at Jassy, the oilfield demolition party learned that a military train was due to leave for Stavka within the next couple of hours. Perhaps more importantly, it was thought likely to be the last train to the Russian Army HQ, where the Bolsheviks were making life ever more dangerous. After a welcome clean-up and a meal, the three men settled down on the train to await its departure.

The journey was surprisingly uneventful, and they managed to secure rooms in the Bristol Hotel in Mogilev, close to the Stavka campus. The following morning, Joe was roused by a persistent knocking at his door.

'Morning, Joe. Time for breakfast.' It was George Hill, arms wide open for a hug. The dining room was humming, but they managed to find a table for two.

'We've got a lot of news to swap, but could you first bring me up to speed on what's happened here? Has my carriage been repaired?'

'It has, and they've made a good job of it. But I haven't moved in again yet. It wouldn't seem right without you.'

Joe gave a short laugh. 'Right, George. We'll move in after breakfast.'

'Maybe not, Joe. I'm afraid you've arrived back to a lot of trouble. A new Bolshevik Council has been set up here and it's demanding that all the foreign missions should be expelled. Worse than that, our friend Krylenko has been at work again, stirring up the more militant rebels and they are threatening more aggressive action, not just expulsion but to kill all members of the missions. They will be calling for this in a mass meeting this morning in the Civic Hall.'

'My God.' Joe was not given to expletives, so this outburst demonstrated the extent of his concern.

'What can we do?' he demanded. 'We can't just sit here. We have to try something.'

'It'll be a boisterous affair, Joe. It might well get out of control - could get very dangerous.'

'Who'll be in control of the meeting? Who called it – the Mogilev Council?'

'I guess so. But the revolutionaries are sure to shout the loudest, and will probably hijack the proceedings.'

'Well, we've gotta give it a go. If I speak to the meeting, are you happy to translate for me?'

George didn't hesitate. 'Sure,' he agreed.

'So what time does this all start?'

George shrugged. 'This sort of thing is pretty haphazard, Joe. I doubt if it's got an official start or finish. If we're going to do this, we'd better get going right now.'

Indeed, the meeting was in full flow when they arrived, and it was already heated with shouting, stamping of feet and waving of banners. Immediately, Joe marched onto the stage and up to the man holding a big gavel, asking him for permission to address the meeting. The man was flustered, being harassed from all directions, and pushed Joe aside roughly.

But Joe was not a man to be dismissed so easily. He moved in front of the Council's table and snatched the microphone from its stand.

'Silence,' he roared. Without waiting for any translation from George, 'Silence' he repeated again and again. It was perhaps curiosity that started to rip open a degree of hush from the crowd, and Joe filled it immediately, 'I am Canadian and we are comrades,' he shouted. George's yelled translation was greeted by a mixture of stamping feet, angry jeers and even some derisive laughter, but it did help to quell the clamour another notch.

'Let me tell you a story,' began Joe. He paused to allow George to translate and for another small hush before launching into a potted history of his pioneering work in Alaska, the taming of the harsh wastes. Gradually, the audience started to listen, shushing any neighbour who continued to shout.

Suddenly, Joe switched his discourse to a history of Russia's brave fights against aggression. Ever since the Mongol invasion in the thirteenth century, Russia had successfully repelled invaders. Poles, Swedes and Napoleon had all attempted to overthrow Russia but had been rebuffed. And now it was the turn of Germany, attempting to dominate Europe. 'And right now, they are occupying Russian land in the south and east.'

His mastery of manipulating an audience was having an effect and his voice became louder and louder, 'What are you going to do about it? You are not quivering mice. You are men - proud Russian men. I command you to force the German invaders out.'

He then began to chant, 'Germans out. Germans out. Germans out…'

It was a mighty gamble, but it began to work - slowly at first, then picking up in volume until there was a steady chorus of 'Germans out.' It was not unanimous, for there were still hardened revolutionaries who supported the change of policy, but it was sufficient for the man with a gavel to realise that their call for foreign missions to be sent home would probably fail, and he managed to close the meeting, still turbulent.

Joe and George were carried along by the crush that followed. Back in the Bristol Hotel, his performance was applauded loudly and the various missions agreed to work together to foster the Allied cause and silence the pro-German agencies.

Joe decided to return to the comparative peace and safety of carriage 451 and, together with George, spent the rest of the morning stowing their stuff in the refurbished compartments. After a pleasant "welcome back" lunch from Ivan, Joe made a start on the backlog of reports delayed by all the recent activities. The two returned to the Bristol hotel for dinner, only to find the remaining missions in "end of term" party mode. They had jointly decided that Joe's intervention had only delayed the inevitable, and they would all be leaving the following morning.

The hotel bar had only ever offered a very limited range of drinks, but it had chosen this night to announce that it was very close to being dry. This had prompted individual members of the various missions to dig into their suitcases for their precious private supplies which resulted in an odd, and potentially lethal, bill of fare ranging from bootleg French eau de vie to some particularly vicious Balkan vodka.

'George, you know that Scotch I bought for entertaining. Would you mind getting it from 451?' Joe was practically tea-total himself but thought they should contribute something to the evening. He had run away to sea in his teens and, during a particularly boisterous time ashore, had drunk himself into such a paralytic state that he swore he would never touch another drop. He had mellowed with age and, although he maintained a lifelong hatred of smoking, he did allow himself the occasional small tipple, especially on such an evening when it would seem unsociable to refuse.

'Aye aye, Sir,' said George. 'How could I possibly refuse a senior officer so immaculately dressed? I'll get it if you'll finally get around to telling me the story of that uniform.'

'Get along with you, you insolent youngster,' Joe responded with a smile. 'It's not that interesting anyway.'

He was pleased to see Steve Locker there - but made no move to greet him because the man was very much the worse for wear from the lethal mixture of unaccustomed beverages. Inevitably, however, he spotted Joe and lurched towards him with arms outstretched for an unavoidable bear hug. He then took Joe's right arm and lifted it aloft, shouting haltingly in a painfully slurred voice, 'Silence. Silence, please. I want you all to know that this is the greatest wartime leader since Alexander the Great, and I have had the honour of serving under him.' Joe, thoroughly embarrassed, smiled and turned away, but Steve caught his arm and whined sadly, 'Joe, my hero...' But his hero had heard enough and pushed himself roughly away saying, 'You've had enough to drink, Steve. I'll catch you later.'

In the morning, Joe found himself waking on one of the sofas in the hotel's reception area. A few lucky ones had kept their rooms on, but the rest were spread uncomfortably over various items of hotel furniture. Others were beginning to stir, and a buzz of conversation was starting up. Word began to circulate that a train had been organised to take the

89

missions to Moscow. Happily, Joe believed this might suit him if he could get his carriage attached. During snatched moments, he had been working on a plan to improve Moscow's suburban ring of stations, and he needed to make on-site inspections before he could submit his recommendations.

'I'm so sorry about last night, Joe.' It was Steve.

'It's OK, Steve. It was a toxic mixture of drinks.'

'It was. But I'm ashamed of myself.'

'It's completely forgotten, Steve. What are you going to do now?'

'I'm staying here as part of the rearguard - tidy up loose ends. I'll keep reporting to London on the situation here. It's changing all the time.'

'Well, good luck, Steve. And thanks for all your great help. I'm not sure what I would have done without you.'

As they said their goodbyes, Steve made one last remark, 'I don't quite recall all I said in my little outburst last night, but I did mean the substance of it. It's been great to know you, Joe.'

'You too, Steve. Go well.'

That afternoon, on the long train journey to Moscow, Joe caught up with more of his reports. He added further good words about Steve to his previous dispatch on Tarnopol, along with commendations on the work of Colonel Chris and Sergeant Sam.

Over the next few days, he attempted in vain to work up a scheme to improve the city's railway system. It had evolved over the years as a series of independent lines approaching Moscow from all directions, but mostly terminating in the outskirts where land was cheaper and more available. But he soon found that his initial vision of extending these lines into the city centre would be far too costly, particularly at this moment in time. Whole swathes of buildings would need to be demolished and new bridges constructed over the mighty Moskva River. Apart from a few minor new suggestions, his earlier efforts would have to suffice for the moment.

Meanwhile, George had been muttering for some time about returning to Petrograd, still the seat of government housing the majority of the country's decision-makers. With his report now submitted, Joe was happy to agree and was just about to arrange for his carriage to be hitched to the Petrograd train when an unexpected visitor crashed through the coach's open doorway and reset all their arrangements for the coming weeks.

Chapter 10

Not often witnessed, a diplomat who has lost his cool is a sorry sight. Breathless from his efforts to climb aboard, the man stood panting for a few moments in the doorway, leaving its two occupants staring in amazement.

'Colonel Boyle?' he finally managed.

'Yes.' Joe identified himself.

'I'm sad to enter like this,' he said in heavily broken English.

'What can I do for you?' asked Joe quietly.

'I not know how to see you,' he started, 'but it is better perhaps - away from embassy. My name is Marcu Diamandi and I am Rumanian Ambassador here. I am very worried and do not know what to do. I ask perhaps you help me.'

'Tell us your problem, Mr Diamandi.'

The Ambassador was clearly in a highly anxious state but managed to pull himself together sufficiently to set out his immediate worries. Rumania was a small country, he explained, currently being overrun by the might of the Central Powers. Before Bucharest fell to the Austrian Army, some of the country's most valuable treasures were taken by train to Moscow and stored for safekeeping within the Kremlin walls. Of particular concern were the Crown Jewels. Not only were they extremely valuable, but they were the history of the country and held a special place in the hearts of all Rumanians. Four large steel cases were brim-full of state crowns, tiaras, sceptres and jewelled swords and were accompanied by several tons of gold bars.

Perhaps of less interest, but still important, was a substantial part of the country's paper currency reserves, confidential government archives and a large and very much needed stockpile of reserve Red Cross medical supplies.

They were still there, but now in grave danger. The new Bolshevik government was already showing signs of throwing the country's fortunes in with the Central Powers, at a stroke making Rumania the enemy of Russia. The Bolsheviks would be sure to get their hands on this treasure. Poverty and starvation had brought his little country to its knees and this, he exclaimed, 'would finish it completely. It is a disaster and I cannot face it, but what to do?'

The two men had listened intently to the sorry tale and could well understand Diamandi's distress. Joe was particularly moved and, as Diamandi was talking, he had visions of the Rumanian countryside with its emaciated farmers scratching the poorest of livings from the land. How might they help to restore these treasures to the desperate country?

'You say these valuables are held in the Kremlin?'

'Yes,' he said brightly, perceiving some interest in his plight.

'Don't get your hopes up too much. I have great sympathy, but I'm not sure how we can help.' After a short break he continued, 'Mr Diamandi, I am curious. What on earth possessed you to seek me out for help.'

'It is a long story, Mr Boyle,' he started. 'I will make it short for you. It was my Godson who is English, Steven Locker, you know him? He told me of some good actions you made in my country.'

That would go a long way to explain Steve's interest in Rumania's plight, thought Joe. 'OK. But how did you find me?'

'This carriage. He could describe it well to me.'

Joe smiled widely. 'You chose well, Sir. I don't know what I would have done without Steve. Now, tell us more about it. Who is in charge of it all? Who would have the authority to release it to us?'

The Ambassador thought for a couple of seconds. 'Me. I believe I do.'

'You need to be sure.'

'Yes. I am.'

'The keepers in the Kremlin will surely want orders for their release, signed by some sort of Russian Official. Do you have someone you can persuade?'

After some deep thought, Diamandi said, 'No. Not really. The Bolsheviks are in charge now. I do not have one in my pocket yet, if that's what you mean.'

'If this is to have any chance of success, Diamandi, it will need some very precise planning. We need full details of exactly where all this stuff is held, how well it is guarded, how we gain access to the Kremlin, and how many wagons will be needed to convey it - so many questions. Without answers to them, we can't begin to make a plan.'

Diamandi looked chastened and thoughtful. 'I have many friends and contacts in the previous regime. I can get this information from them, I believe. No time yet for much change in Kremlin I think.'

'OK. I'll start organising transport and try to get some sort of Government authority for its release. You prepare one on behalf of Rumania - preferably with a Royal signature.'

Joe stood up and moved towards the Ambassador. 'Then I want you to get as much information as possible on precisely where and how it's all stored, and we'll meet again here in two days to see if we can come up with a watertight plan. Without one, I'm certainly not putting my life at risk.'

He turned to his friend. 'I don't know if you're prepared to join in with this enterprise, George, but do you agree with all that?'

As George nodded, a big grin appeared on Diamandi's face.

'Oh thank you, gentlemen. Thank you. With you two in charge, I am sure valuables will be saved for my country.'

'Don't get ahead of yourself, Mr Ambassador. There is a long way to go before we can even agree to help you.'

'I understand,' he said as he prepared to leave. 'I will be here in two days - 11 o'clock.'

Without saying anything, George naturally threw his lot in with Joe as he busied himself with the extensive preparations. Joe's first call was to Moscow's Kommandant, who he was heartened to learn was still Valerie Muralov. The two men had struck up a good relationship in the short time he had been in Moscow and he felt that his success with the railway system might have earned him a favour or two.

'Joe. Good to see you again,' said Muralov as he gave Joe a bearhug, quite a normal Russian greeting he understood. 'I've been following some of your exploits. You certainly know how to mix things up, although I'm not always sure which side you're acting for.'

'For whichever side I consider to be in the right, Valerie,' said Joe. 'Given all the circumstances at the time,' he added.

'Good man,' declared Muralov.

'I've been looking at your ring of suburban stations - sent you a report on them a few days ago.'

'Thank you for that, Joe. I saw it - but very briefly. It's with Nicholai now.'

'Valerie, I have a favour to ask. It's more than a little delicate and I hope you will treat it as confidential between the two of us.'

'I can't promise anything, Joe - as you can well imagine. But I promise to listen.'

'You're going to need some of the pragmatism we've just been talking about.'

'Sorry. I don't know that word, Joe.'

'It may not be the right word anyway. I mean, to think out of the box - not necessarily along party lines - to do what is morally right.'

Joe went on to outline Diamandi's history of the Rumanian valuables locked up for safekeeping in the Kremlin. The change of government in Russia has made Rumania very nervous. It is a very poor country, much of it already under enemy occupation, and cannot afford to lose these items.'

Muralov listened attentively while Joe carefully chose his words.

'The Rumanian Ambassador has made a formal request for their return and I am considering how I might best approach the authorities in the Kremlin. I do hope you will agree it's the correct thing to do, Valerie, and I would be most grateful if you could assist me?'

'Wow. That's some request, Joe. I have no idea who has that sort of authority.'

He went into a deep reverie. After a minute or so he said, 'I'm not even sure any permission is needed. If Rumania has deposited items for safekeeping, they can surely be withdrawn on request.'

'That's precisely my view, Valerie.'

'Right, I'll simply sign a note giving you free passage to enter the Kremlin, load up the deposited items and return them to Rumania. Will that do?'

'I could wish for nothing more. Many thanks, Valerie.'

'I would tell as few people as possible, Joe. Russia is a dangerous place today, full of bands of ruffians and revolutionaries. I assume you will take them by train. It'll be a long journey.'

'I agree,' said Joe, 'discretion shall be the watchword.'

Joe was delighted at the outcome and tucked Muralov's note into a fresh file he had opened. Meanwhile, George had been making himself useful by seeking out a carriage company where horses and wagons could be rented at short notice.

The following day, Joe set out to reel in some more goodwill. He called in unexpectedly on Nicholai, the City Engineer who had helped him run the Union meetings that had kickstarted the improvements to the Moscow railways. He was bowled over by the greeting he received, Nicholai embracing him like some long-lost brother. This promised well for the favours he was about to seek, and indeed he had no trouble organising Carriage 451 to be attached to the following Monday's southbound train, along with some extra carriages for the archives and medical supplies.

Diamandi did not dampen these encouraging moves when they met up the next day. He had even managed to enter the Kremlin to view the treasures. The Kremlin is essentially an immense enclosure for palaces and cathedrals built over the centuries in a variety of styles. General security was provided by a small garrison whose Commander was also responsible for the management of a variety of ancillary buildings, including numerous stores. This post was frequently gifted by members of the Royal Family, and the new Bolshevik Government had probably made Captain Boris Vasiliev feel somewhat insecure in his position. Diamandi judged him to be honest, if fairly ineffectual.

The Red Cross medical supplies were by far the most extensive and Diamandi thought it may be impossible to include them all. The Crown Jewels were held in a separate storeroom but, after examining his records, Diamandi discovered that he held a key as part of the contract. Everything seemed to be straightforward enough and they settled down to decide on the remaining details. Fewer people were likely to be around the city centre on the day of worship and Joe had already decided that Sunday should be the day for pick up and loading, ready for the train the following day. Eventually, all was agreed and, as the meeting broke up, Joe impressed on all of them the need for complete secrecy.

A light dusting of snow greeted the early risers on Sunday. At the chosen entrance, the driver sat with a scarf wrapped around his face against the biting wind. Muralov had arranged their entry and for them to be escorted to the Guard Office where they found a small group of soldiers commanded by a Sergeant. Quite possibly the ugliest man in the world and with the body of an ox, his demeanour was immediately aggressive. He did order his men to assist in the loading process - but not out of any desire to help, simply to ensure that items were removed in the order he dictated. Nothing, he insisted, should be removed from the locked vault.

This was highly disturbing, and when Diamandi asked to speak with Captain Vasiliev, he was told that he was not normally on duty at weekends and would probably be in church. The Ambassador insisted that he be called in, but it took a threat by Joe to get Muralov out of bed before the Sergeant reluctantly agreed.

'What is the problem,' the Captain demanded on arrival, rather testily.

'Your Sergeant is obstructing the loading of the wagons,' Diamandi said, 'and he won't allow items in the vault to be removed. I have the key.'

The Captain turned to look at his Sergeant, simply lifting his chin to demand an explanation.

'We've heard rumours, ' he began. 'We've heard there are items of great value stored in that vault.'

'So? Everything in there is included in the schedule of deposited goods. I have checked.'

The Sergeant looked at his fellow soldiers for support. 'We're at war, and that's expensive. The Revolution has lost us loads of money too. The country is broke, and we could do with the extra funds this treasure could provide.'

'So you're suggesting we confiscate it, eh?' said Vasiliev, shaking his head. 'How would anyone trust us if we are reduced to acting like that with our allies? No, I have no idea what's in those cases, but they will remain locked and returned to their rightful owners. Is that clear?'

'Very good, Sir.'

Joe, who had been looking on anxiously, was greatly relieved. Whatever else he was, the Sergeant was a lifelong military man and would not disobey the orders of his Officer. When Joe had set out to get the support of Muralov and his Chief Engineer, he had been careful to avoid mentioning the Royal Jewels or gold bullion. It helped too that the original contract's schedule referred to them simply as "a variety of Royal appurtenances". It is therefore quite conceivable that any knowledge of the jewels was merely the stuff of rumour.

For sure, Captain Boris Vasiliev had won the day for them. But what none of them knew was that he had already glimpsed the contents of the cases during a routine security inspection. He knew of its huge value and had no intention of allowing the State to appropriate this windfall - not whilst he harboured a bold plan of his own for its next destination. The first element of his plan called for the treasures to be freed from the secure confines of the Kremlin walls and, before he left for his Sunday roast, he was assured this would be taking place early the next morning.

In the meantime, whilst George continued to transport the remainder of the consignment, Joe took some meticulous measurements of the cases that held the jewels, and then went shopping.

The following morning did not start auspiciously. A row had blown up concerning the constitution of the train, the driver asserting that the carriages containing the files and medical supplies should properly be classed as goods and it was illegal to couple them up to the passenger coaches. Leaving Joe to sort this out, George headed for the Kremlin to pick up the final load.

Diamandi was waiting at the gates, but he was not alone. A squad of Rumanian soldiers came smartly to attention as George approached.

'What on earth is this, Diamandi? We agreed to keep this operation low-key, a secret.'

'I'm sorry,' he replied, more than a little embarrassed. 'My government insists that the valuables must be protected by an armed guard, travelling with them all the way. The Prime Minister himself telephoned the decision to me.'

'That's ridiculous,' shouted George, 'If word gets out, how do you think twelve men could see off a determined group of soldiers or Bolsheviks?'

'I know. I did explain it all to him, but the decision's been taken and he won't budge.'

'I don't fancy your chances of survival when Joe sees them. He's going to be furious.'

George turned and walked through the gates. 'Let's just get on with it,' he shouted back contemptuously.

Back on the train, a few roubles soon settled the dispute with the driver and Joe set about preparing his new purchase to receive the Crown Jewels. An ancient oversized sea chest, he was confident that it would not look out of place in the compartment when its flat top was suitably decorated with books, a few photographs, and perhaps even some flowers. It was secured by three wide leather straps and a heavy iron lock from which an enormous key currently protruded. As he admired his purchase, Ivan appeared with a cup of coffee and a biscuit. He pointed at the chest and raised his thumb in approval. Not for the first time, Joe regretted his inability to talk to the man and tell him of their mission. He must himself have led a life full of adventure, and would surely approve. He resolved to get George to take him into their confidence and show him that we trusted him as part of the team - a trust he had already demonstrated on several occasions.

Noise from outside told Joe that the goods had arrived and he went out onto the entry platform to greet them. His smile disappeared instantly as his eyes caught sight of the military escort, marching along either side of the laden wagons. Over the next few seconds, his face reddened and the veins in his neck stood out, throbbing. He was clearly about to explode.

Seeing this, Diamandi decided to make a pre-emptive attempt to defuse the explosion. 'My government insists,' he said as firmly as he could manage.

But Joe was not to be placated so easily. 'What the hell are you doing with a fucking guard advertising the operation?' Joe's dislike of swearing once again betrayed the strength of his anger. When George told him that they are due to remain on board the train throughout the journey, he pronounces angrily, 'Like fucking hell they are.'

Joe's voice was interrupted by a long shrill whistle announcing the train's imminent departure. 'Come on,' he urged. 'We'll be off soon. Let's get all this stuff stowed away.'

Some of the cases were heavy and it became a struggle to lift them to the level of the train floor. Diamandi sought out Joe and apologised once again for the escort. He was profuse in his gratitude to the two men for taking on his cause and wished them a speedy and uneventful journey. Then, with a brief wave, he was gone.

Left on their own, the two men set about loading the sea chest. Joe's measurements proved accurate and the Crown Jewels fitted with space to spare. It was whilst they were packing in some of the gold bars that a violent lurch told them that their journey to Rumania had begun.

Chapter 11

Joe returned to Dawson to find that Frank Slavin had left the Yukon to make what he could from boxing. Having wasted several months waiting for Sifton's decision, Joe could not afford to let this delay consolidate his grip on the town's infrastructure. Resolutely clinging to his sweeping concessions, he built a power station which would provide energy for his future dredgers and bought into the local telephone service. He had two sawmills constructed and along the riverfront, added a 200-foot wharf equipped with lumber hoists and warehouses. He was already a major player in town and "Soapy" was forced to curtail some of his excesses and to work with him.

His success did find resentment and opposition in some quarters. Miners who had previously cut down trees for free suddenly had to pay for processed timber. He learned to balance his commercial activities with generous improvements to local amenities. He provided public street lighting throughout the whole town and a new slab road to be laid along the length of Main Street whose layer of thick mud had rendered almost impassable.

All these activities he managed to finance from profits in his New York freight business. But to pursue his vision of the future, he next had to seek the fresh eye-watering finance he would need. He found himself juggling his time between Dawson and the rest of the world. In Ottawa, New York and London he spent months at a time mingling in courtrooms and boardrooms with Guggenheims, Rothchilds and others. He also opened discussions with the Marion Steam Shovel Company in Ohio, USA for the design and construction of his dredgers, blueprints for which already existed from machines at work in other goldfields. With all this movement, he was greatly assisted by improvements in travel to and from the goldfields. By the turn of the century, steamships were plying the upper reaches of the Yukon River and a rather precarious single-track railway was constructed along the path of the White Pass that Joe had earlier trailed.

It was not until 1904 that the first of the giant dredgers began its year-long journey from Ohio, a tortuous new route to the goldfields almost doubling the prime cost. First shipped to the mouth of the Yukon River in the Bering Sea, the massive components were transferred to flat-bottomed barges and painfully slowly pulled by paddle boats upriver to Dawson. A natural-born longshoreman, Joe was in his element. Seemingly diminished in stature by the giant buckets, sieves and girders, his dwarfed frame barked out orders in his deep sonorous voice as he supervised every leg of the journey to the Klondike. In Dawson, the miners marvelled at the sight of the giant components being unloaded and arranged in orderly rows, ready for assembly. It would be several months before the finished beast was ready to launch.

Although only the first and smallest of Joe's dredges, it was still an awesome sight. Standing some 100 feet tall, its sixty-seven buckets, each weighing nearly two tons, were poised to gouge out and process huge mouthfuls of gold-bearing river bed, around the clock in half-decent weather. Most of Dawson turned out to watch it take its first faltering steps and Joe paid Frank Slavin's fare to be with him on the day. A friend of Joe's, the young poet Robert Service, wrote of dredge Number One.

"And turning round a bend I heard a roar,
And there a giant gold-ship of the very newest plan
Was tearing chunks of pay-dirt from the shore.
It wallowed in its water-bed; it burrowed, heaved and swung;
It gnawed its way ahead with grunts and sighs;
Its bill of fare was rock and sand, the tailings were its dung;
It glared around with fierce electric eyes.
Full fifty buckets crammed its maw; it bellowed out for more."

Joseph Whiteside Boyle had now truly earned his title, "King of the Klondike."

Chapter 12

It was a long and heavy train, hauled by an aged engine that made ridiculously slow progress. Classified as a post train, it was not expected to reach its destination in less than six days. Trundling through the snow-covered countryside, it stopped occasionally for a new engine driver, water, fuel or simply an exchange of passengers. This was frequently chaotic with hundreds of people from all walks of life, from farm labourers to doctors, royalists and revolutionaries, all clamouring for spaces inside the carriages, many left hanging from the running boards or spilling over onto the roofs. Joe's carriage was safely locked, but the roof had to be constantly defended, quite often using force.

At the last minute, the troupe of Rumanian soldiers had been crammed into the carriages carrying the files and medical stores. They had been desperately uncomfortable, with almost no provisions, and after several hours their officer had taken it upon his own initiative to declare the accommodation uninhabitable and they quit the train at one of the stations.

At Bryansk, the sound of gunfire alerted Joe who then awoke George. The driver ramped up the speed as the train approached the station, which was the scene of a pitched battle between Royalist and Revolutionary forces. Sprays of bullets from indiscriminate rifle and machine-gun fire thudded into the carriages injuring many of the passengers - particularly the poor devils lying flat on the roofs. Joe's carriage, being bulletproof, was spared all but a few dents and a couple of shattered windows, and the train sped on for a couple of miles before settling down to its previous sedate pace.

That night, Joe was on duty when the train began to slow down. Looking out, he could see a fire ahead and, as they approached, the cry went out throughout the length of the train that it was a vodka factory. This was nectar from the Gods for the engine crew who immediately stopped the train, and for the passengers who began to swarm across fields to the blazing factory. They returned clutching as many bottles as they could carry. Some of them, unable to wait, smashed off their necks and poured the clear liquid into open mouths. With a lot of drunken behaviour likely, Joe woke George to double up the watch. There were no major incidents as the train slowly chugged onwards for the next couple of days which allowed the men to catch up on paperwork, George on his field journal and Joe on his reports and letters.

However, they immediately smelt trouble the next morning when the train came to a halt in a dilapidated wooden building and was surrounded by Bolshevik troops with a Commissar at their head. George went forward to investigate and reported back to Joe that all the carriages were being thoroughly searched.

Joe saluted the Commissar as he entered their carriage, 'Welcome, Commissar. But I'm sorry, you cannot bring your party into this carriage. We are a Foreign Mission and are not subject to search.'

The Commissar hesitated, but only for a short moment. 'I have orders to search every carriage, Colonel.'

'You will be violating international conventions if you do. Our country, and others too, will never forgive you.'

'What is your country?'

'Canada,' said George, pointing to Joe's badges.

'Is that the American Republic?'

'Yes,' replied George, unwilling to argue the point.

'I'm sorry. I have my orders. It is believed that there is some treasure aboard this train and, if it is true, I must find it.'

'Treasure?' exclaimed George. 'What are you talking about? We are simply returning some Rumanian documents to Jassy. The Russian authorities know all about it. Joe, do you have Muralov's letter of authorization?'

'Certainly have,' declared Joe, reaching for his briefcase.

'I'm not interested,' said the Commissar in a firmer, more confident voice, 'I have my orders from a higher authority.'

He turned to Joe, who was seated firmly on the treasure coffer. 'You are a military man, Colonel, you must understand that.' George didn't bother to translate as the Commissar broke off to oversee his men carry out a thorough search of the carriage. For a moment, it looked as though they might have got away with it, but the Commissar suddenly turned to Joe and demanded, 'What is in that chest?'

Joe sat tight as George answered with a shrug, 'Just more documents, Commissar.'

'Open it, please.'

'Oh now, Commissar. These documents are highly confidential. This Mission cannot let you see them.'

Drawing his pistol, the officer barked an order and the air was suddenly filled with the sound of clicking bolts as bullets were loaded into a dozen rifles. Joe and George looked at one another helplessly. The Commissar jerked his gun at Joe, ordering him off the coffer. Reluctantly, Joe slipped off and stood aside.

The leather straps were removed and two soldiers vainly attempted to open the padlock.

'Where is the key?'

'We don't have it,' said Joe. 'I think it must be held in Jassy.'

The Commissar cocked his gun and went up to the lock to shoot it off.

'Oh. I remember where it might be,' shouted Joe, not prepared for the jewels to be shot to pieces. The gun remained trained on the lock as George talked to Joe, who then delved into the right-hand hip pocket of his uniform and handed the key to the Commissar.

George continued to put up resistance as a soldier unlocked and removed the padlock but, as the lid was slowly lifted, his voice trailed away and he stepped forward, mouth wide open, as bundles of paper files stared up at him. Joe calmly took one out and, looking at the Commissar, spread his hand over it to indicate that it was confidential and not for his eyes. The Commissar appeared to accept this but lifted a couple of bundles to ensure that nothing was hidden underneath. He nodded, re-holstered his gun, and said briefly, 'Thank you, gentlemen,' and left the carriage followed by his men.

For the next half hour, only a few sly grins passed between the two men until, with a couple of wild lurches, the train resumed its journey.

'Well?' demanded George.

'I'm sorry, Podge,' Joe replied, using a nickname he had come to use at key moments. 'Ivan and I thought of a better hiding place. I decided we should take him into our confidence. I know that the man is a fierce Royalist, and he's taken the safety of the Crown Jewels as his personal responsibility. He'll kill for them.'

'Well, he's doing a great job. Where are they then?'

'They're in a void space behind some cupboards in his pantry. During the first bloody purge of the revolution, he hid a couple of kids there for more than a week. They were Princes, sons of Empress Marie Feodorovna, the previous owner of 451.'

They were now past the halfway mark and the next morning pulled into Kiev, a picturesque town, once the ancient capital of the Russian Empire. Joe wanted to rest up for a couple of days but was startled by the Station Master's opening remark.

'I hear you are carrying a great treasure with you, Sir. Why are you doing so without an armed guard?'

'Nothing of the kind,' Joe assured him, laughing at the thought. However, on learning that a different train would be leaving for the Bessarabian frontier that night, he issued orders for their carriages and wagons to be attached to it. They had all been living in the same clothes for a week and the two men agreed to take turns guarding the train whilst the other had a bath and a meal. George drew the first straw and at the Continental Hotel met an old friend, well-decorated in the Russian Chevalier guard, who was on his way to Bessarabia. Seeing value in having the services of an additional reliable man, Joe agreed to Captain Nabakov joining them in Carriage 451.

In the afternoon, after his bath and meal, Joe went off alone to a meeting at the South-Western Railway HQ. It lasted longer than expected and, on his way back to the train, he ran into a street skirmish where a bomb exploded close to him. The blast blew him through the window of a provisions shop where he lay senseless for several minutes amongst a variety of cuts of meat and vegetables. When he did come

111

round, the shopkeepers were very solicitous, plying him with brandy and insisting that he lay still to recover. They spoke no English, of course, and even the most inventive hand signals failed to get them to understand how important it was that Joe leave immediately for the station. He looked at his watch, only to learn that the train should have already left. He began to panic, but the good people continued to insist that he must rest.

It was almost Christmas Eve and Joe spotted a large cooked turkey lying on the kitchen table. He sat up defiantly and offered to purchase the bird. This flummoxes the couple and, perhaps believing that he was by now fully recovered, she wrapped up the turkey and let him go.

Meanwhile, at the station, George had been imaginatively trying to delay the train's departure, all three warning bells having sounded with a no-show from Joe. He asked the Station Master to delay the departure of the train for 15 minutes which was agreed reluctantly, but as 8.15 passed there was still no sign of Joe. George decided that their carriages must be uncoupled but, with little chance of another suitable train, he was determined to hang on until the last possible minute. He engaged the good Station Master in conversation but, as the clock reached 8:30, the man got up and said firmly, 'The train is now leaving.'

George went to the back to ensure that their carriages were uncoupled when it was Ivan who came up with a technical suggestion that once again saved the day. George called out to the Station Master who was already threatening with a green flag in his hand.

'Hey, we have a problem here. We have no emergency stop. It's really important.'

The emergency stop system onboard was simply a cord running through eyelets on the outside, and this had not been extended to our additional carriages.

'We do appreciate that you're anxious to get the train off, but surely safety is paramount. It must be against regulations to travel without a full security system in place?'

The Station Master, already marked as a stickler for rules and regulations, hesitated for just a moment before pronouncing that the system must be re-strung, and it was nearing the end of this process that a breathless Joe arrived and clambered aboard clutching a large parcel. As the train finally left for Bessarabia, the Station Master smiled and waved, clearly content with his day's work. The men settled back in their carriage, confident of a less stressful time on the next leg. Joe didn't voice his fears, but he was considerably more sceptical.

A day later, as they left Ukrainian territory, his fears grew stronger. Something was wrong. It was all too quiet. With no Commissar waiting at Jamerinka, just forty miles from the Rumanian border, Joe sensed trouble ahead and alerted the others.

Less than twenty miles from the border, the train stopped at Vapniarka and a nervous Station Master announced, 'This train ends here. It will be shunted into a siding, and there will be no further trains through Bessarabia today.'

The passengers soon realised that he was serious and gradually left the train, complaining bitterly as they faced a difficult onward journey.

Joe was furious and sent George and Captain Nabakov to demand an engine. As they began to leave the carriage, a man sporting the insignias of a General pushed past them, accompanied by his staff. At first, Joe felt he was witnessing some sort of bizarre joke. Was he expected to take this music hall act seriously? Resplendently garbed in a uniform of bright red and gold, the General's chest was festooned with a bewildering array of medals, crosses and stars, the man was surely dressed for the stage. But his jaw was set firm and his iron face bore no signs of comedy.

'You are all under arrest,' he said brusquely.

'You must be mistaken,' George protested. Joe fished Lenin's mandate from one of his uniform pockets and handed it to the General who scanned it briefly before handing it back with a contemptuous shrug of the shoulders.

'We are trying to aid the revolution. Here, I have a similar warrant from the Moscow Commander …' But the General interrupted, waving aside Muralov's authority.

'How long will this last?' asks George. 'When will we be allowed to leave?'

'I have no idea. Maybe never,' said the General firmly. 'I believe you are stealing something from Russia to give to Rumania. This cannot be allowed, and you will not be permitted to continue your journey. Your Mission is covered by two batteries of artillery just 500 metres away. They have orders to open fire if there is any movement of the train.'

Shocked, Joe tried to defuse the situation. 'Sit down, General. Let's have some tea and talk about this.'

'No.' The man sounded exasperated. 'I'm serious. I mean what I say. Any movement of this train and it will be destroyed.'

A new face suddenly appeared at the carriage door. Yet it was a face that Joe instantly recognised as Captain Boris Vasiliev, the Officer in charge of the Kremlin Guard. Joe groaned inwardly as he began to see the light. These were no Bolsheviks. The General's dismissal of the words of Muralov and Lenin bore witness to this. And no Royalist possessed the authority to mount such an operation. No - this was a personal smash-and-grab assault on the Crown Jewels by Captain Vasiliev, no doubt calling on the assistance of the mock General and his "rent a mob". Another thought, the Commissar who had earlier carried out an abortive search of his carriage was almost certainly also in on the conspiracy. How else would he have known about the treasure? Joe now realised that a considerable array of adversaries posed a significant threat to his mission. This was reinforced a moment later when Vasiliev stepped forward.

'So we meet again, Colonel Boyle. But under very different circumstances.'

He was enjoying himself, his very presence ruling out any denial of the treasure. 'I am aware that an earlier search failed to find the jewels, but the man was too weak. I know that they are hidden somewhere on this train and I can assure you now, gentlemen. We will find them.'

He took one short step forward and spoke assertively, 'Starting tomorrow morning, we will begin stripping down this train, section by section, panel by panel until they are revealed. We will not leave here without them. And you, my friends, you in the meantime will all remain prisoners in your carriage. A guardhouse will be set up in the station and, as the General has already announced, two batteries of Howitzers are even now trained on your carriages.'

115

A new approach was called for and George cut in quickly. 'I thought you might have guessed by now, Vasiliev. The jewels are not on this train. They were transferred to a different, faster train some days ago - at one of the earlier stations. They'll be in Rumania by now.'

This brought a smile, more like a sneer, to Vasiliev's face. 'You think we're amateurs, don't you? You'll soon learn that we're not. We are professionals - military men like yourselves. We have had scouts on the train, and we're quite certain that nothing was transferred at any station. The jewels are on this train, and we will find them.'

He started to move away, then hesitated and turned to Joe, looking him up and down. In a heavily accented attempt at English, he began an unlikely offer. 'I guess you're in charge here, Boyle. You seem a reasonable sort of man. It would save a lot of time and upset if you would tell us the location.'

'You've got to be joking,' Joe retorted immediately. 'Go fuck yourself, Vasiliev.'

Whether or not he fully understood all of Joe's angry words, he certainly caught the spirit.

'I didn't think so,' said the Captain and then added, 'Why can't you just accept the inevitable? You are fortunate that we are not ourselves Bolsheviks, who by now would doubtless have already resorted to many bizarre and brutal methods of making you talk. Even so, I cannot promise to avoid such measures if we continue to be thwarted.' After a short pause to let his threat sink in he continued, 'I'm certain the jewels will not be hidden on any of the regular passenger carriages, so that section of the train will shortly be setting off back to Moscow. That will leave you and your carriages stranded and entirely at our mercy.'

116

Joe had long since dismissed the pantomime General as some ridiculous attempt to gain their attention and not as one of the main conspirators. Vasiliev was unlikely to wish to share the prize with many accomplices, he thought, and quite possibly only the friend who had earlier searched their carriage, masquerading as a Bolshevik Commissar.

More pieces of the puzzle fell into place as Vasiliev gathered his troupe to move out. 'We're leaving you in the good hands of Sergeant Dimitrov. He commands my crack team of guards who are currently setting up their quarters in the station offices. He's a good man if not crossed but with any nonsense, he can turn into a beast from hell. Be warned. I won't be far away, with my father here, at the site of the Howitzer battery.'

'Your father!' Joe exclaimed and gave a little laugh.

Vasiliev smiled and shrugged his shoulders. 'He has always hankered for the grease paint. I hope he didn't scare you too much. Now - I don't believe you'll cause any trouble. You won't want to leave without the jewels so you can wander about outside. But I suppose we should disarm you. Will you please place any weapons you have on that chest?'

As the three men unholstered their guns, Vasiliev continued, 'And also any hidden in the carriage, please. If we find any when we take the carriage apart, we'll use it to execute you,' he added with a smile.

Joe went into his bedroom and came out carrying a wooden case which he handed to Vasiliev. Looking surprised, he opened it slowly and took out an ancient-looking firearm.

'Duelling pistols,' exclaimed Vasiliev. 'Very nice too. Have you used them in anger?'

'I haven't,' replied Joe. 'My father did. I inherited them from him.'

'He won the duel then.'

'No. He died.'

A moment of silence, Vasiliev looking confused. 'I'm sorry,' he queried.

'The pistols belonged to my father. His killer had once been a great friend of his and was an honourable man. Later, on my 18th birthday, he sent the pistols to me.'

Vasiliev sighed as he placed the gun back in the box, carefully closed the top and handed it back to Joe. The silence that followed was punctuated only by the regular belches of steam from the engine.

'You can keep these,' he said. 'I don't believe they present any danger to my men. I just hope you will be sensible enough to survive the next 24 hours.'

As he left with his entourage, the carriage was suffused with a pall of doom, their efforts being frustrated at the very last moment. There seemed little they could do and settled to play piquet to clear their minds. But as the hours slowly passed a feeling of excitement formed in the pits of their stomachs, as of the moments before a battle. These were men of action and each one realised that some form of aggressive action was needed - and needed soon.

Chapter 13

A nearby whistle and burst of steam told them that the passenger coaches were leaving for Moscow, and they revived the flickering flames of a plan that had been smouldering in Joe's mind.

But first, they would have to reconnoitre the site to get a good idea of the layout of the station and the likely capabilities of their guards. Joe reckoned these would most likely be regular soldiers under the command of Captain Vasiliev, and probably knew nothing of his intrigue.

Joe decided to get some air. He and George stepped down into the station yard and, with no sentry intervening, they continued to wander into the extensive sidings. It appeared that Vasiliev's words about their freedom of movement had been extended into his orders to the guards. But they were certainly being watched from a distance and it would no doubt be a different matter if they started carrying cases of treasure.

The sidings were littered with goods wagons, many already loaded with timber. To Joe, this raised the possibility of some form of utility engine somewhere on the site, and they set off to search for it in a relaxed saunter to avoid attention. Joe was aware from his experience in Tarnopol that it is common practice to keep an engine permanently with steam up in case of need at short notice. Seemingly, the practice had never been stopped at this station and they soon came across an old shunting engine in a shed behind the station offices.

Two men in blue overalls were sitting in front of an open coal stove sipping some sort of brew from metal mugs. Assuming them to be the driver and fireman, Joe pushed George gently by the elbow to join them. He didn't want a guard to be dispatched to investigate their disappearance, so he stepped back into their view and started doing some physical exercises. In a loud whisper, he primed George, 'Gain their trust. Get them to talk about themselves. Find out if they might be open to doing a job for us. You know the sort of thing to offer - lots of money, anything they seem likely to want.'

It was almost twenty minutes before George emerged to recount his negotiations to a tiring Joe. The two men were utterly disaffected, being treated abysmally by the railway authorities - unpaid for several months. Both were Bessarabian and their families close to the point of starvation. They only kept going because there was no other work to be had. 'Having told them briefly what we wanted from them, they were wavering with the money I was offering but my final shot was to offer Rumanian citizenship. They jumped at that like jackrabbits, and I'm certain that they're now firmly onside.'

'Good. Well done, George. I've been firming up my plan whilst I've been waiting. We're going to have a party this evening - soften up the guards until we're ready to make a break for it.' With some relief, he wound down his exercise. 'On a scale of one to ten, George, how reliable are these guys going to be, do you think? We don't want to build up an elaborate plan only to be let down at the last minute.'

'More than nine certainly. I doubt if they've experienced the current conditions in Rumania, but they're very keen to get permission to live there. I'm certain they'll show up.'

'We'd better explain to them precisely what will be required then.'

'So far, I've told them we're on a secret mission for the Rumanian government and are being held prisoner by Bolshevik rebels. During the night we want them to very quietly roll their engine up to hook to the three coaches in the station and make full speed for Jassy.'

'Ok. Go back and tell them that the break-out is planned for 3.00.am exactly. Make sure they know to keep hidden away until then. Emphasise that we will be completely reliant on them, waiting on the train for the engine to be hooked up. And tell them, good luck.'

George nodded their acceptance as he returned, and they wandered slowly over to the office where the guards were quartered, all the time taking in the displacement of the guards currently on duty. As they approached, the Sergeant opened the door and stood with arms akimbo, clearly refusing entrance. But Joe wanted to assess their communication capabilities, and how they would get word to the howitzer batteries. He would try another track, George translating.

'I thought we should meet, Sergeant.'

'Sir?' he acknowledged respectfully.

'Well. We're both prisoners really - us in our carriage and you in here. It can't be very comfortable.'

'I've known worse, Sir.'

'The only real difference between us is weaponry. You've got lots, both big and small; we've got none. We can be no threat to your security, can we? So you can relax, eh.'

'Captain Vasiliev said the same thing, Sir.'

'So, can we come in? I'd like to chat with your men.'

'Sorry, Sir. They're off duty and, as you say, relaxing.'

'Could I please speak with your Captain on the telephone?'

'No, Sir. I'm afraid that won't be possible.'

'Why on earth not, Sergeant?'

'No telephone set up, Sir.'

'You surely don't have any radio yet?'

The Sergeant snorted a laugh. 'No, Sir. No radio.'

George sounded baffled. 'How do you communicate then?'

'We have our ways, Sir.'

Having established that their guards were not in telephone contact with the heavy guns, George considered that he should not probe any further. He looked at Joe who nodded his agreement. The two sites were not very far apart and perhaps they simply relied on runners. As they readied to leave, George mentioned that they had expected to be in Rumania by now and had planned a party to celebrate. To pass the time, they proposed to keep to the plan. There would be some singing and vodka if they would care to join them.

'We'll see,' was all they got from the Sergeant, although the mention of vodka must have been attractive.

Back in 451, Joe decided to lay out his plan in detail to his comrades in arms. He knocked at Captain Nabokov's compartment, but there was no reply. Trying the handle, he found it had been locked. Again he knocked and this time heard a strangled grunt from inside.

'Captain, I'm calling a meeting about tonight's action. Are you Ok?'

'I'll be out in a minute or two,' responded Nabokov breathlessly.

The incident sent Joe's mind into overdrive as he returned to the main compartment. He had never taken much to the Captain, who rarely joined in with their activities. Now, he had taken to locking himself into his quarters. What did he have to hide?

And where had he been? He sounded extremely breathless as if he had been running some distance. It crossed Joe's mind that he could have visited Vasiliev whilst he and George had been out. Could he possibly be a part of the conspiracy? He would speak to George and watch his every move closely.

Once the three of them were together, Joe told Nabokov of the engine he and George had discovered. As Ivan served them tea, he told of his meeting with the guard Sergeant.

'They don't seem to have immediate communication with the Howitzer batteries, so we might have a reasonable run if we can get away quickly. There appears to be only a single door from the guardhouse. If only we had just one gun, we could perhaps keep them pinned inside for a while. Otherwise, they'll be out in force as soon as the alarm is raised and we'll just have to duck and take it. And that's why we're going to have a party tonight. George and I managed to come away with quite a stash of vodka from the burning factory and, if we can get them a bit pickled, it might take the edge off their accuracy. Needless to say, we'll be going easy on the booze, eh.' He paused to let that sink in.

'Anyway, it'll pass the time. And we'll put on a bit of a show too. I have no musical instrument to play and my repertoire of jokes doesn't include any in Russian, but I do sing a little. What about you guys?'

'I'm not a member of the Magic Circle, but I could do a few conjuring tricks,' announced George, somewhat sheepishly.

They turned to Nabokov, who hesitated for a few seconds. 'I'm no showman. But I do know some popular Russian songs. Might get them going.'

'Excellent,' said Joe. 'That's settled then.'

At that moment, the three heads turned with mouths that began to open wide as an extraordinary apparition appeared at the kitchen door. Ivan was dressed in a highly decorative, but unknown, uniform complete with multiple rows of medals. And in his hands, outstretched in presentation, he held an ancient rifle of some description.

'Ivan,' was all Joe could manage to exclaim.

The man looked suitably proud as he spoke in Russian. George and Nabokov both laughed, which seemed to slightly annoy Ivan. George turned to Joe and translated. 'He reckons he'll be able to keep the guards holed up in their rathole.'

'You shouldn't laugh,' Joe chided them. 'I've seen what old-timers can do with a single-shot rifle. If nothing else, he might well be capable of delaying and confusing them.'

Nabokov reached out and examined the gun closely. 'It's an old Berdan, isn't it? Breech loaded, very reliable. If he's any good, he should be able to get a round off every 5 or 6 seconds.'

Joe turned to his faithful factotum. 'Spasiba, Ivan,' he said, virtually exhausting his knowledge of the man's language. At the same time, he gave a thumbs-up approval of his offer.

'Right,' he said to George, 'tell him we will be leaving at 3.00 am. He should be in position a few minutes beforehand - the signal box would give him some cover and have a good sight of the guardhouse door. And suggest that he wears something a bit less colourful.'

'We'll start the bash at 8.00. In the meantime, rest up and rehearse your party piece.'

Throughout the meeting, Joe had been watching Nabokov's reactions. His face showed no signs of the excitement that might be expected from such a proposal. Indeed, he appeared rather gloomy about the prospect, beads of sweat glistening on his forehead. Why was this? Was it the possibility of the scheme failing? Or was he perhaps thinking of how he could inform his co-conspirators of the plan?

When the meeting broke up, Nabokov left for his compartment allowing Joe to float his concern to George.

'How well do you know Nabokov, George?'

'Not particularly well. Over the last couple of years, we've run into each other from time to time. He's a dour sort of fellow, not easy to get to know very intimately. Why?'

'I've become quite worried about his motives for joining up with us. Two or three things have made me wonder if he's perhaps another of the conspirators.'

'Good Lord,' exclaimed George. 'What on earth has given you that idea? '

'When we got back from our tour of the yard, I found him locked in his compartment and he took ages to open up. When he did, he was sweating and out of breath, as if he'd been running. But where, and why? And this afternoon he showed no relish for our escape plan, all the time looking worried and sweating copiously. I can't work it out. Something's wrong.'

'Hmm. I hope you're wrong, Joe, but I'll keep a close eye on him.' After a short pause for thought, he continued, 'Now. If you don't mind, I'll go and practise some tricks for this evening. I'm more than a little rusty.'

Left to himself now, Joe decided to take his own advice to rest up. Sat in his favourite armchair, he went through his extensive repertoire of songs in his mind, picking out what he considered the most appropriate for the situation. It wasn't long though before the events of the last few hours took their toll and he fell into a deep sleep.

And he was still asleep when, as darkness began to fall, a figure dressed all in black slipped silently from the train and headed towards the lantern hanging outside the guardhouse.

Chapter 14

Joe was awakened by the clink of glasses. Ivan was preparing the room for the party and a glance at his watch told him that his curtain call was only some twenty minutes away. He fully expected to kick off the proceedings himself, but it was unlikely to be the sound of his voice, however pleasant, that would attract the Sergeant and his men, so Ivan had set up an enticing display of vodka bottles. It was fortunate, Joe thought, that vodka was as clear in appearance as the water in his own glass.

In the event, it was less than a quarter of an hour before half a dozen soldiers were hanging around the open doorway.

'Come in,' said George. 'It's far too cold out there. Come in and grab some vodka.'

They didn't need a second invitation and the affable Sergeant led in about half of his troop, leaving outside just one miserable-looking armed guard. Joe was in the middle of one of his favourite Irish ballads, but little attention was being paid as each accepted a tumbler of vodka with apologies from George, 'Sorry about the large glasses, fellas. They're all we have.'

Joe decided on a change of mood and started on some popular songs of the day, songs like *Polly Wolly Doodle* where the lyrics are irrelevant the world over. It made little difference to these men, however, who continued to chat and laugh as they began the serious business of drinking. As he looked at their craggy faces, old and new, he soon realised that his repertoire was unlikely to hold their attention and beckoned Nabokov to take over.

To give him his due, the Russian jumped straight into the spirit of the evening and a real party mood soon took a firm hold. The soldiers sang along with Nabokov's drinking songs and swapped jokes, most of them probably smutty. George's conjuring went down well amid roars of laughter and he was forced to repeat his routine when, after an hour or so, the Sergeant swapped around his men for those who had remained on duty. He felt security was sufficient enough to remain on board himself.

All evening, Joe's misgivings about Nabokov remained, but he could see no signs of any connection or familiarity with any of the soldiers.

It was almost midnight before the Sergeant felt it was time to call a halt to proceedings, politely thanking his hosts. He had not drunk excessively himself, but he realised that a couple of his men were more than a little worse for wear. When the soldiers had all left and the room cleared up, there was nothing to do but wait for action at 3.00 am.

Joe soon began to wish he had made it earlier. With more than a couple of hours to ponder the possible dangers, Joe's mind inevitably began to scrutinise the various elements of his plan. He soon began to realise how very fragile it all was, every part of it needing to work exactly as planned. And even then…

But what was the alternative?

Critically, could the engine crew be relied upon? For without their success, the whole escape attempt would die in its tracks. He had not studied the yard's marshalling layout so had no idea of how they would link up with 451.

Joe was heartened by the sound of a friendly wind that had got up. It had led to a low background grumble from a variety of loose pieces of railway equipment and might have helped to disguise the engine's movement.

The two Howitzer batteries did worry him. Without a telephone link, the guards would surely have another way of calling for them to fire. What was it, and could he stop it in some way? They would need a quick getaway, Joe decided, but before any other possible problem could enter his mind, he fell into another welcome sleep.

'Half an hour.' Joe awoke abruptly and slowly took in George's words. The action was now only a whisker away, and they must ready themselves.

'I'll make sure Nabokov is awake,' George said and left the room. But only a few seconds later he shouted for Joe. Nabokov's door was once again locked and he didn't reply to calls. Ivan, dressed in black overalls, appeared and explained that there was no lock, but the door had been secured by an internal latch that should be capable of being broken. George took up this suggestion and stepped back as far as possible in the narrow corridor to kick hard at the edge of the door. It gave at the first attempt with a splintering of wood and opened to reveal the Russian Captain, also dressed in black, lying motionless on the floor.

Joe rushed forward and knelt to check for signs of life but, before he could do so, the man moaned and began to sob gently.

'He's shell-shocked,' George said confidently. 'I remember now. He was a survivor of the horrific battle of Tannenberg at the beginning of the war. I believe he was fortunate not to be charged with cowardice but was eventually removed from active service. He must be simply terrified by the thought of the big guns trained on this train.'

'That must explain his trips away from the train. He was trying to find a way out.'

'I guess so,' agreed George. 'Poor chap. But there's nothing we can do for him right now. Let's just put him in his bunk.'

As they left, Ivan was climbing down from the train with his trusty rifle slung around his body. George wished him a whispered good luck and he disappeared into the deep black of the night. There were only a couple of dim bulbs glowing in the train, the only other light on the whole site being the lantern outside the guardhouse, gently swinging in the wind.

Tension rose as the minutes ticked by, but then was suddenly lifted by a gentle lurch of 451 as the engine snuggled up. Joe silently thanked the two railmen who were on time and apparently without raising any alarm.

But then a shot by Ivan rang out and all hell let loose.

A soldier was seen to fall in the doorway. But while Ivan was reloading, the Sergeant stepped over the body and raced out into the yard brandishing a handgun which he fired a couple of times, not at the train, but into the sky.

With urgent belches of steam, the train began to move forward and, as it began to pick up speed, the night sky suddenly became day. Of course, realised Joe, why hadn't he thought of it before? This was Vasiliev's improvised method of communication - flares. It provided an instant order to open fire, at the same time illuminating the target area.

Another soldier was seen to stumble and fall as Ivan kept up his pressure. But others scrambled out swiftly and began shooting at the train as it moved clear of the station. His job done, Ivan left the signal box and started to run for the train, his rifle bouncing on his back. A distant boom, followed by a whining screech announced the arrival of the first shell which exploded amid a small string of goods trucks, sending them reeling in cartwheels.

The soldiers stopped in their tracks and stood around in confusion, looking at each other. They were not going to reach the train now as it began to enter the long bend clear of the station, so the Sergeant decided for them to withdraw to find some cover.

Ivan was running at top speed, his rifle swinging wildly from side to side, to catch the rear carriage. He was almost there when another shell exploded behind him and Joe saw him sprawl forward just as he became obscured by the bend.

By this time, shells were beginning to rain down. But the train was approaching top speed now and was separated from the guns by a dense cover of trees. The only direct indication of its position was the billowing puffs of smoke from the engine, hardly visible in the dark. Both range and accuracy were poor and the crippling explosions were falling increasingly behind the flying train.

'I do believe we've done it,' shouted George.

'Careful...' Joe warned against tempting providence.

And with good cause. With distance ever-increasing and the shelling gradually fading away, it was easy to believe that good fortune had been showered upon them. Yet they were still some distance from the Rumanian border.

132

Chapter 15

'Something of a miracle though,' suggested George, the euphoria of their apparent escape persisting.

'Yes,' agreed Joe. 'We were very fortunate. I can't help thinking about Ivan though,' said Joe. 'I have visions of him caught by an explosion just as he was about to board.'

'I know,' agreed George.

'Perhaps it was too dangerous. I know how much he wanted to help, which he certainly did, but maybe I shouldn't have accepted his offer.'

'I don't think he would have appreciated that,' George said.

'No. Probably not,' said Joe. 'But what if he was wounded? If the guards found him, I think they'd treat him well. The Sergeant seemed a reasonable fella. But they probably left pretty quickly, in which case Ivan could be lying injured and unable to move.'

After a moment's thought, he continued, 'We'll organise a rescue party when we get to Jassy. We should be there in an hour or so.'

Adrenalin was running far too high to attempt any more sleep and Joe decided to write up the story of their escape.

'Before you do, don't you think this is a good opportunity to tell me about your uniform? It's not quite as theatrical as Vasiliev's toy General, but it's an oddity nonetheless.'

'You got me, George.' He paused, gathering his thoughts. 'I was in Alaska when war was declared, and almost immediately felt that I had to do something positive. I had made a small fortune in the goldfields and, with the start of the winding down of exploration, many fit young men were looking for work. I'd been impressed by a demonstration of these new machine guns, and I decided to raise a detachment of around forty soldiers, train them and send them to Europe. It was in recognition of this that, when I arrived in London, I found I had been gazetted by Ottawa as an honorary Lieutenant Colonel in the Canadian Militia.'

'I was chuffed when I was given this job and decided that a uniform would give me added clout when dealing with foreign leaders. In discussions with Grieves and Hawkes, we settled on a slight variation of the British pattern. As you've seen, on the shoulders are *'YUKON'* badges in black, a cap circled in red braid and a badge in pure Alaskan gold, and lapel badges of maple leaves fashioned from the same pure gold. I've got three sets and wear them most of the time. That's it. Satisfied?'

'Yes.' George smiled. 'I can't imagine you without it now.'

'Well, just go and rest up while I get on with this report. We'll be in Jassy before long.'

But George didn't care for any more sleep. 'We were talking of Ivan's courage. It's an odd thing – bravery in the face of death. I don't know if one is born with it, but we've seen it sadly lacking in Nabokov. Maybe it was there all along, but simply knocked out of him by his terrifying experiences in the course of battle.'

'I believe everyone is scared at the point his life is threatened,' said Joe. 'It takes true courage to continue in the face of it.'

George carefully picked up the wooden box that Vasiliev had allowed Joe to keep and was still lying on the great chest. 'It's a beautifully made box,' said George. 'May I?'

'Go ahead.' Joe nodded with a smile.

As George opened the box he continued, 'Duelling is a case in point. How must it have felt – the two of you standing just a few feet apart, ready to be shot at? It must have taken a lot of guts.'

'Indeed,' agreed Joe. 'and if for any reason the pistol failed to work, it couldn't be reloaded and you could do nothing but stand still and wait for your opponent to take careful aim and fire. Family rumour has it that this is how my grandfather died.'

George took one of the pistols out of the box. 'I assume they work like any other single-shot gun.'

Joe held out his hand to take it. 'I'll show you.'

He took out a substantial metal flask. 'Gunpowder,' he said, tapping a quantity of the fine black granules into the muzzle. 'It has a smooth round bore - no rifling.'

Next, he took out one of the large lead bullets and slipped it into the muzzle. 'They're heavy,' Joe exclaimed. 'Nearly always fatal, often several days later.'

He delved into the box once again and produced a small ramrod and tamped the bullet firmly onto the bed of powder. 'There are other bits and pieces, including some replacement flints,' he said, rattling a tin.

'When the hammer is cocked, the pistol is ready to fire. Pulling the trigger releases the mechanism that rasps at the flint and causes a spray of sparks to ignite the powder. Hopefully,' he added.

It was as he added this word of caution that the train suddenly screeched to a shuddering halt. George was thrown backwards in his chair and ended up against the carriage wall. Joe injured his ribs as he was thrown violently forward into his desk amid a shower of loose objects flying around him. Jumping up, he ran to the entrance platform

135

just as lights were switched on to illuminate the scene. He saw that the train was now surrounded once more by armed soldiers, but not in the same uniforms worn by the Russian soldiers. Looking around for someone in charge, Joe caught sight of an officer hurrying from the front of the train. As he drew near, he began shouting in an unrecognised language.

George pushed past Joe saying, 'I think they're Rumanian. They might well understand Russian. Let me try.'

The exchange that followed established that the man did speak Russian, and indeed had a smattering of English. He announced that the train had reached the Rumanian border. With the rapid decline in relations with both Bessarabia and Russia, his Squadron had been hurriedly deployed to deny all access by train. To facilitate this, he had arranged for a full wagon of earth to be dumped on the track, although their engine had fortunately managed to stop within the first two or three feet and so had narrowly avoided derailment. With George translating, the officer stepped forward and introduced himself.

'My name is Lieutenant Popescu, and you can go no further. How many people are on board, please?'

George answered, 'There are three of us, plus the driver and fireman. You must let us through, please. We are on urgent business, known to Prime Minister Bratiano.'

The soldier appeared to wince at this and stood still for a few seconds before continuing, 'What is the nature of your mission?'

'We are returning to your country a mass of confidential files, emergency medical supplies, and some belongings of the King and Queen.'

136

'Where have you brought them from?'

'Moscow,' replied George.

The ramification of this news was not lost on the young Lieutenant, but his ponderings were suddenly interrupted by his Sergeant who had been searching the rear coaches and now reported what he had found.

'So far as we can tell, your story seems to be true. But what's this about the Royal Family's possessions?'

'That's a private matter I'm afraid. You'll have to trust me on that.'

Popescu paused for thought. 'OK,' he said finally, 'I'll telephone HQ for orders.'

This would take some time and Joe decided to return to his carriage. As he turned, his attention was hijacked by an extraordinary sight. From the rear of the train, a ghostly apparition was advancing toward him. At first, almost completely obscured by dense billows of steam, the thin frame of a man very gradually became a recognisable figure.

'Ivan,' exclaimed Joe excitedly, jumping off the platform and running towards him with open arms. George followed immediately, congratulating him on his escape. Becoming the centre of attention was not easy for the shy man but he managed to explain what had happened. He had felled a couple of the guards and prevented others from leaving the guardhouse. As soon as the train had begun to get up speed, he had slung his rifle around his body and sprinted to catch it up. Almost immediately, a shell exploded behind him, the blast throwing him forward onto the ground. He had scrambled up, apparently not seriously injured, and took up the chase once again. Aware that his rifle was slowing his progress, he reluctantly threw it aside and ran for his life.

He was lucky. The train was travelling quite fast now around the bend that marked the end of the platform. Just as his breath was giving out, he managed to put on a little extra burst of speed and throw himself at a handrail attached to the back of the last coach. Clinging on, he used his very last ounces of strength to clamber into the now speeding train and collapse onto a pile of files. He lay there for some time, recovering his breath and giving thanks to God. He knew that there was no communication between the end carriage and 451 so decided to stay put, not wishing to attempt a trip over roofs at night on a speeding train.

The next thing he knew, he had been thrown to the floor by the violently breaking train. Not knowing the reason for the stop, he decided to await developments. After a while, he came face to face with the Sergeant who seemed friendly enough and simply looked through a couple of the files. Jumping down from the train he slowly moved forward until he could make out the conversation between George and Popescu, learning that it was safe to emerge.

'Well done, Ivan,' said George. We have been so worried about you.'

'No one can catch Ivan,' he said proudly, and before long was tidying up the shattered kitchen in advance of preparing some breakfast.

This great news was followed rapidly by some more as Popescu announced that he had received orders to let them through. They didn't have any mechanical plant so it would take some time to manually remove the earth. Once he had arranged this, he climbed aboard and shook hands with Joe and George, congratulating them on their successful mission. He told them of the excitement that their arrival had caused within the Rumanian government.

But all trackside celebrations were suddenly cut short by the arrival of a large staff car sporting a powerful spotlight that dazzled the surprised party. During the final leg of their journey, Joe had caught glimpses of lights that appeared occasionally some distance from the train, wondering perhaps whether they were being shadowed. He had kept the fear to himself, but it was now confirmed as the tall figure of Captain Vasiliev stepped forward from behind the light shouting,' Who is in charge here?'

He was immediately followed by a couple of burly soldiers with rifles at the ready. Joe guessed that they had been with the group of Howitzers and had set off from there as soon as the flares had raised the alarm.

'Speak up. Who is in charge?' Vasiliev bellowed.

Popescu looked confused, having no knowledge of this new arrival, and turned to George and Joe for advice. But it was this movement that alerted Vasiliev to their presence.

'Ah!' he shouted. 'I believe I need look no further.' As he did so, an Army lorry appeared and, as it slid to a halt beside Vasiliev's car, it disgorged his remaining soldiers. Popescu's troops were still holding shovels, separated from their guns so that the Russians held a clear advantage in the standoff that ensued.

Vasiliev had put aside the mocking smile he had worn earlier and he addressed Joe sternly. 'So, we meet one final time, Colonel. I am pleased to see that your men are already equipped to dig your graves. That is indeed an encouraging start.'

'You are no longer on Russian soil, Captain. These are Rumanian soldiers charged with escorting this train to Jassy, and we will be expected there shortly.'

'Nonsense,' exclaimed Vasiliev. 'I am not leaving without what I came for. I am certain now that it is somehow distributed or hidden in your special carriage and my men will strip out all equipment from the bedrooms and kitchen.' After a short pause he continued, 'We will find it, I promise you.'

As he spoke, he moved towards Joe whose face remained unmoved, his feet set square and hands clasped behind his back.

'Remove your pistol and place it on the ground in front of you. Slowly now, Colonel. Do nothing stupid.'

Joe's hand appeared from behind him and he unbuttoned the holster. Slowly, he lifted out the revolver and threw it onto the ground in front of Vasiliev who, with his own gun trained all the while on Joe, bent to pick it up. As he did so, in one swift movement, Joe's other hand emerged holding the duelling pistol which he immediately discharged into the top of Vasiliev's head. The heavy lead shell instantly shattered his skull with its contents exploding such that those close by instinctively closed their eyes and ducked to avoid the shards of bone. When they looked again, Vasiliev's headless body had toppled to the ground and was bleeding out, his gun having fired harmlessly into the earth. Many of them immediately closed their eyes again, unable to look at the terrible sight, but Joe's eyes remained on the Russian Sergeant who had wisely held back on any instinctive reaction.

He shook his head slowly as their eyes met. A million thoughts must have run through the man's mind as he weighed up how his next move might affect the rest of his life. Finally, he lowered his rifle and snapped to attention. Joe will never know whether this was a gesture of submission or to honour the death of his Commander, but it was followed by a series of orders in Russian whereupon his men lowered their weapons and headed for their truck. Before following them, he remained for a moment and spoke again in his mother tongue, translated by George, 'I was never sure what this mission was all about,' he began. 'There was talk of some treasure and I guessed it was some sort of private venture by the Captain. Whatever it was, it ended with his death, and we'll be heading home to join up with whatever is left of the Russian Army. We'll take the Captain's body with us. With all the carnage around, it shouldn't be difficult to construct some heroic story of his actions against the rebels.'

George stepped forward to reply. 'You're a wise man, Sergeant. Good luck to all of you.'

Within five minutes, they were all gone. George started to explain the backstory to Popescu whose men had belatedly begun to retrieve their rifles. He marvelled at the exploits and urged his men to speed up the earth removal.

Joe settled down in 451 to write up the day's momentous events whilst they were still fresh in his mind only to be interrupted by George who had once again decided that sleep was out of the question.

'Now. Was that an act of inherited bravery or extreme stupidity,' he demanded.

Joe pursed his lips. 'Hmm,' he murmured. 'I have no idea.' George realised that this reply ended any further discussion on the subject of bravery.

'I could see no good outcome. We'd been caught napping and it seemed that I alone had any form of primed weapon, albeit only the dodgy duelling pistol we had loaded. I cocked it behind my back and offered up a prayer. I knew I would have just the one chance but, so long as the dammed thing worked, I couldn't miss – he was so close.'

'You're a very brave man, Joe.'

'Or stupid,' Joe responded with a rue smile, 'it ended well enough, although I hate taking the life of a young man.' He paused for a moment's thought, then, 'We should be on our way soon.'

A sliver of light on the horizon announced the arrival of a new day as the train rolled warily over the remains of the obstacle to begin the last hour or so of their epic journey.

When it finally reached Jassy, Carriage 451 drew to a stop beside a hastily gathered welcoming party, surrounded by some cheering early risers. The Rumanian Foreign Minister and Railways Minister were already in place as Prime Minister Bratiano breathlessly worked his way to the front. Joe and George received a rapturous welcome as they jumped down from 451 and Bratiano, in a short speech, indicated that King Ferdinand would be conferring honours on them later in the day.

Joe suddenly broke ranks, sprinted to the engine and dragged the driver and fireman from their cabin. Standing between them, he raised their arms in triumph amid delirious applause from the crowd. Not to be outdone, George leapt aboard 451 once again to extract Ivan from his kitchen and lead the reluctant man to join the party. Both men had visited Nabokov during the last lap of the journey and found that he had managed to find some degree of composure, but they were happy to accept his wish not to be included in any celebrations.

As the cheering began to subside, the welcome party broke up and work began to remove the currency and jewels to secure locations, Joe ensured that his promises to the engine driver and fireman would be honoured and that Ivan was being well looked after. He then joined George on 451 which they decided should remain their home whilst in Jassy. After polishing off the remainder of Joe's turkey, for the first time in ten days, they could undress for a welcome hot shower and change of clothes.

There was to be no state banquet to celebrate the occasion as the royal couple lived quite modestly in their temporary residence in Jassy. But an audience for the two men was arranged for that evening and they talked, thankfully in English, for more than half an hour. Joe recounted their adventures on the train and told of their meeting with Bolshevik leaders at the Smolny Institute and their fears that Russia may pull away from the Allies.

Queen Marie marvelled at their exploits and thanked them 'from the bottom of my heart.' Later, she described the meeting in her diary 'I had a busy day. I had to receive a very interesting Englishman, a certain Colonel Boyle, who has been working for us in Russia trying to better our situation. A very curious fascinating sort of man, who is frightened of nothing and who, by his extraordinary force of will and fearlessness, gets through everywhere. The real type of English adventurer about which books are written.'

She had been told that he was Canadian earlier in the evening, but from the very start, her mind seemed to have linked him with her own country of birth. It could have been the similarities in the uniform, but it might also have been the sign of an immediate attraction. And when they came to leave, and the Queen extended her pale slim hand for a kiss, Joe too may also have experienced a meeting of the senses that he would share with this beautiful lady.

Chapter 16

Dawson City had seen a big change. 'Soapy' Smith had been killed in a gunfight and residents could tread the streets at night without fear. The relief that was felt had introduced a mood of moral respectability with gambling and prostitution becoming banned. To compensate, Joe introduced sporting diversions, including boxing and ice hockey. In a covered, but somewhat ramshackle arena, Joe trained up an amateur team to challenge for Canada's most prized sporting trophy, the Stanley Cup. Composed mostly of local talent, they played a series of three matches against the mighty professionals of Ottawa and were hopelessly outclassed. Nevertheless, the Yukon Nuggets captured the imagination of the nation and remain to this day a legend in the history of the national sport.

Whilst not without numerous forays into the courtrooms of the world, Joe settled down to comparatively sedate life in a large new house in Bear Creek, several miles from Dawson. To the relief of his ageing parents, his children joined him along with his brother who took over the lumber side of the business. One neighbour, in particular, became Joe's lifelong friend, and it is Teddy Bredenbergh's son, Chris, who takes up the story.

"I remember the incessant noise from the dredges, the screeching whine of metal followed sometime later by the loud thump as the craft lurched forward in its pool.

But I also recall a very happy childhood - lots of us children having fun together in a huge natural playground. Every year, Joe Boyle would take us kids for a picnic with fun and games. A piano was loaded onboard and Joe would lead a sing-song all the way home.

In the evenings, the house was always full of grownups. Robert Service frequently came over from Dawson where he worked in the bank. He would read his poetry which Joe would memorise and later recite to relatives in Ireland and to royalty in Rumania.

Joe loved all animals and supported a veritable zoo. Herbert Hoover was an engineer before taking up politics and on one visit presented Joe with a pair of white Aberdeen terriers, referring to his host as "a picturesque and lovable Irishman." Their enclosure was often left open and the animals would frequently be seen wandering around the house. I recall one occasion being summoned to the big house. Joe had taken to his bed for an afternoon nap and was a sight to behold. Awake now, he was lying with a big grin on his face. On either side of his head lay asleep Hoover's two white terriers. One of the lynx kittens was asleep at his feet, the other lay on the floor. The only animal awake was the brown bear cub who was licking the hairs on his bare chest."

By now, Joe had amassed a small fortune. His first wife, Millie, whom he had never divorced, had worked her extravagant way through Joe's generous settlement and suddenly turned up demanding a share of it. Hoping for an improved deal, she sued for divorce but was very disappointed when she was awarded alimony of just $50 a week.

But the divorce made Joe a highly eligible bachelor, vulnerable to the many gold diggers of the female variety. It was a surprise, therefore, when he returned to Dawson one day with Elma Louise, a manicurist he had met and married in Detroit. She was a gentle, demure little homemaker who should have married a successful city businessman for a peaceful domestic life. Not Joe Boyle.

Because Joe, who was now approaching fifty, was about to embark on a new, even greater, series of adventures. It was 1914 and the awful word rang out in the Klondike's hills and valleys - "War!"

Joe stood looking out onto Bear Creek. His first dredge was out of sight now, around the bend in the river. The mountains of tailings it had left behind added nothing to the view and he wondered, not for the first time, how they could be improved. He disliked the idea of leaving the Yukon so sullied.

His concentration was broken. "Where the hell are you, Joe? You're surely not on this planet."

He smiled as he turned towards his friend, "Hey, Teddy. No. You're right. Except I was thinking of this planet - and I'm worried about it."

"I was thinking too of the war in Europe. This Kaiser's built himself some really powerful forces, and if he does manage to annex all of Europe, where then? The world will be at his mercy."

Teddy Bredenberg said nothing, perhaps a slight nod of the head.

"I have to be involved, Teddy. I'm too old to fight on the battlefields, so what can I do?"

"I dunno, Joe. I'm very fond of England, as you know - got lots of friends there. I'd love to help them too."

"I've been thinking about it over the last few weeks, and I've started things off. I was in Cleveland a couple of years ago and saw a demonstration of one of these new machine guns. My God, Teddy, they're scary - they can shred a man in a couple of seconds."

He paused, still thinking. "Anyway, I've decided to throw some money at it. I've been talking to Sam Hughes, the Defence Minister, and he's agreed to my offer to finance a Yukon fighting squadron. It'll be about 50-strong and based on the machine gun. I'm told it will form a detachment in the First Canadian Machine Gun Corps."

Teddy was beaming. "Joe. That's great. Well done." After a short pause, "That's going to cost you a packet though."

"I know, Teddy. But I have money now. Just lying in the bank simply makes Henry Rothchild richer. I can make it work."

The Dawson theatre was overflowing as Joe set out his proposal and, with the slowing down of gold prospecting in the Yukon, it was already oversubscribed by the time the last man left the meeting. What started as a motley collection of characters were drilled by members of the Mounted Police and by huntsmen for shooting practice. After just one month, with the winter fast approaching, Joe decided that any further training should be carried out abroad and ordered up a steamer to take them on the first leg of their long journey to war.

A huge crowd turned out for their send-off, where Joe presented them with a mascot - a husky dog named Jack. The recruits were praised to the skies by local dignitaries and a short speech by Joe left hardly a dry eye. He then led the whole contingent down to the dock, the new soldiers with their kit bags on their shoulders. Hundreds of well-wishers joined in with the singing of "Pack up your troubles" and then "Tipperary." As the midnight departure time approached, Jack led the troops aboard in a torch-light ceremony, the band struck up, and the whole of Dawson stood ramrod stiff as "God save the King" was played.

The euphoria of that night was blunted a few days later when No. 2 dredge developed a serious fault and sank. Attempts to raise her proved difficult and dangerous with one sailor killed and many others seriously injured. Eventually, all efforts failed to bring her back into reliable service and she became an expensive write-off. This accident probably exacerbated Joe's growing disenchantment with life in the Yukon. His company, the Canadian Klondike Mining Company, was by now a mature business with all the major problems a thing of the past. With the action now in Europe, he decided that he was wasting his time in Alaska.

Joe felt confident enough to leave the management of his company to his brother, Charles, and his son, Joe Jr., who was by now a qualified engineer.

Then, he packed his bags and went to war.

Chapter 17

The following morning, in sharp contrast to the previous day's excitement, the demolition party found Jassy to be the saddest of places. The ancient city was doing its best to host both Government and military headquarters but was overcrowded and overwhelmed. Surrounded by enemy forces and with little road or rail access, there were few deliveries of any provisions and many were dying daily from starvation.

Joe did not stay long in Jassy as a meeting with Prime Minister Bratiano landed him a new assignment. Russian rebels were threatening to overrun what remained of Rumania and, knowing of Joe's good relationships with several leading Bolsheviks, he was tasked with negotiating some form of a peace agreement between the two countries.

Joe took Carriage 451 to Petrograd once again where the railway yard Manager welcomed him warmly. He was enjoying the revival in the fortunes of the railways and perhaps even his salary. He professed to have heard only brief fragments of the carriage's adventures over the last weeks and listened in growing amazement as Joe recounted the epic journey with the crown jewels. However, it was not long before he gave Joe the disappointing news that both Lenin and Trotski were away negotiating a peace treaty with Germany. Without one of the top leaders, he feared that he was destined to draw a blank, but managed to wash away his disappointment with a bottle of Chateau Mouton Rothschild to accompany his first decent dinner for some time.

Over breakfast, Joe recalled his first visit to Smolny and, in particular, remembered how Adolf Joffe had greatly impressed him and resolved to seek the man's advice. The chaos that still pervaded the Bolshevik headquarters was at least the result of a meaningful plan, for it was in course of being relocated to Moscow. No longer was entry freely permitted, with armed guards interrogating and frisking all callers. Impressed by Joe's smartly pressed dress uniform, the garrison commander was called who eventually managed to establish his request to see Joffe. He was shown to a small room where he waited for some twenty minutes before Joffe appeared at the doorway, smiling and offering his hand.

'Colonel,' he said. 'How good to see you again.' It was clear that Joe had equally impressed at their first meeting. 'I've read of your exploits - not all of them favouring the Revolutionary cause, I hasten to add.'

Joe guessed he was referring to the funds lost to the Revolution in the heist from the Kremlin walls. He smiled, shrugged and replied, 'They all seemed right at the time.'

'Hmm,' muttered Joffe. 'Anyway, it all makes for exciting reading.'

'Now,' he continued quickly, 'Comrade Lenin has left me in charge here, so my time is very limited. How can I help you?'

'It's very good of you to see me at such short notice, Adolph. I am most grateful.' After only the slightest pause, Joe outlined the brief he had been handed by the Rumanian Prime Minister, with Joffe looking increasingly confused.

'Wow,' he exploded as Joe finished. 'You're after a non-aggression treaty between Russia and Romania. Is that right?'

'There are positive advantages for both parties,' said Joe hopefully. 'Europe is in turmoil and it must be better to know who your friends are. It's surely worth exploring?'

'But the vast majority of Rumania is currently occupied by the Central Powers with whom, as I'm sure you're aware, I have been leading negotiations for an armistice. It hasn't come up yet, but the division of the spoils of war could well result in Russia annexing countries such as Rumania. Why should we disclose our hand at this time? It just doesn't make sense.'

The dialogue had ceased abruptly, Joffe with a knowing smile playing around his lips and Joe painfully aware of the frailty of the Rumanian case.

It was Joffe who broke the silence. 'Anyway. It's not for me to make such decisions. If you're still keen to pursue the case, you'd better speak to Joe.'

'Joe?'

'Stalin. Joseph Stalin. With Lenin and Trotsky both away, he's your man.'

Apart from the fact that he was a member of the top triumvirate in the Bolshevik regime, Joe knew little about the man. But then he recalled that he was the founder and editor of the party newspaper, Pravda - and also something of a villain.

Joffe had been examining Joe's reaction closely. 'Don't worry. He's a pussycat really. Don't let his coarse language put you off, and don't let him get on top. He has a pathological dislike of foreigners, so perhaps you can make use of that.' After a moment of thought, he added, 'I suppose I shouldn't be saying all this, but he's not my favourite person.

He certainly gets things done though, and Lenin rates him. They go way back.'

'He doesn't sound like the flexible sort of man I'm after,' Joe said dismally.

'No. I don't believe he is. But he may perhaps see some merit in your proposal. After all, he's just been presiding over the independence of Finland when many were against it. He's back here tomorrow and I'm sure I can get you ten minutes if you'd like.'

'That would be good,' said Joe, but it sounded very much like a last-ditch effort.

'I must run now, Colonel. I'll get a message to your hotel.'

'I'm in my railway carriage in the yard. The manager will take a message.'

They shook hands and Joffe was halfway through the door before he suddenly turned. 'Joe Stalin gets irritated very quickly,' he started. 'Look out for his moustache. When he gets angry, it bristles and seems to sprout forward aggressively. It's not a good sign.'

Joe smiled. 'Thank you, Adolph. I think I'll be able to manage him,' he said confidently.

The following morning, Joe sent an urgent telegram to Prime Minister Bratiano with a gloomy report on progress. He had arranged a meeting with Stalin but, unless his advisers could come up with more convincing arguments, the possibility of any treaty would be dead in the water. Joe was pleased to receive no call from Joffe that day, as it was late evening before he got Bratiano's reply. Joe was none too impressed with its contents but hoped that something might perhaps spark a whiff of interest.

That night, his mind frequently turned to work on his presentation of these new ideas. But it was during a bout of deep sleep that he was awakened by a loud thumping at the door. He was still in his pyjamas when it was flung wide open to reveal a flustered yard manager waving a telegram.

'This has just arrived by motorbike. You've got a meeting at Smolny in less than half an hour,' he shouted breathlessly.

This was the last thing Joe wanted to hear. One of his greatest pleasures in life was to slowly clothe his body in a freshly pressed dress uniform, finally attaching the Yukon gold accessories and medals. But it was now a race to the line, with no time for such luxurious thoughts.

Joe was shown into the same small room at the rear of the guardhouse. As he sat down on the hard wooden chair, he couldn't help wondering how many cameras and microphones were concealed within the racks of paraphernalia that lined the walls. Expecting to be kept waiting for a while, he was pleasantly surprised when the door opened almost immediately. He was briefly confused by the sight of a spectacled man who bore little resemblance to the photograph of Stalin that he had remembered seeing somewhere.

'I'll be interpreting for you,' said the man as he fetched another chair and sat at the end of the table. 'Comrade Stalin will be here in a moment.'

But as the minutes stretched, the man introduced himself as Slava. 'I fear you would have difficulty with my full name,' he explained. Following some awkward small talk, Joe was interested to learn much of the details of the regime's move to the Kremlin.

It was almost ten minutes before the door was flung open and Stalin strode in. Around ten years younger than Joe, he drew up a chair, placing a conspicuously empty file on the table between them. In stark contrast to Joe's distinctive style, he wore a plain dark grey utility shirt buttoned to the neck. But his most distinguishing feature was his jet-black hair. On his head, it was thick and stood piled up way above his forehead. It was matched by a bushy moustache that obscured his upper lip and had been fashioned into sharp points at each end.

After shaking hands, Stalin started immediately, 'I have read reports of your exploits in our rail system. Excellent work. We are very indebted to you.'

He paused then, before setting the tone for the meeting. 'But I'm afraid the debt is unlikely to be repaid today, for we have no interest in any form of treaty with Rumania. The country barely exists. I'm sorry, Colonel.'

'I'm sorry too," Joe responded. 'As you rightly say, the country is on the edge of extinction and desperately needs help from countries like your own who have much in common. Its population is starving and attempts to find food in Bessarabia are being thwarted by revolutionaries. Rumania holds more than 400 Russian prisoners from this conflict. They have no wish to detain them and some form of agreement is surely needed to exchange them and provide a cessation of hostilities.'

'That may well be,' said Stalin. 'But that is simply a local matter, I'm afraid. It doesn't begin to justify a formal treaty. Volo Antonov is in command down there. I'll give you a letter of introduction. He's a good man. See if you can sort something out with him.'

If Joe considered there was any mileage in continuing the conversation, he was not given the option. Comrade Stalin simply got up, closed the still empty file and hurried out with a breezy, 'Good to meet you, Colonel.'

Somewhat nonplussed, Joe looked appealingly at the interpreter. With a smile on his lips, Slava simply shrugged his shoulders, perhaps offering a little sympathy for the whirlwind he had just witnessed.

'Stay here for a moment,' he said. 'I'll get you that letter. It shouldn't take long.'

George was at Jassy station to greet him the following day. 'I didn't like to say anything, but I doubted you'd have much luck,' he said.

'I'm not giving up yet,' countered Joe. 'As soon as I can arrange it, I'm off to meet with Antonov, the Bolshevik regime's commander of the southern front. I'll take 451, and I'd be grateful if you'd join me. I've missed you.'

When they arrived at Sevastopol station, they found that the town had been placed under martial law. Several days earlier, the sailors of the Black Sea Fleet had mutinied, mercilessly torturing their officers, wrapping them in chains and throwing them into the sea. But now these mutinous sailors surrounded Joe's train and demanded to see the occupants of Carriage 451.

Their leader, a club-footed sailor named Speiro, proclaimed Boyle and Hill to be the advance guard of a British force massing in the Dardanelles, preparing to attack the thinly spread Austrian forces occupying Rumania. His rhetoric had roused the throng which now surged forward threateningly with all the hallmarks of the sort of lynch mob they had witnessed at Stavka.

Joe knew that he needed to gain some time and invited Speiro into his carriage. With George translating, he reeled off a potted history of Turkey's involvement in the war. They were still firmly allied to the Central Powers, he insisted and there was no way they would permit any British force through the Dardanelles straits. It was all a malicious rumour.

But all the time things outside were becoming uglier. Perhaps the mob had become fearful of the safety of their leader, but the more adventurous were now trying to break into 451. Through the window Joe watched one man, stripped to the waist and sweating profusely, swinging a pickaxe at the carriage side. He saw him back away, confused as his hard work simply bounced off the armoured steel plating. A sailor, seated on the shoulder of another, was hammering with a crowbar at the window which was crazing but had not yet shattered. Joe looked at Speiro who, despite looking concerned, merely shrugged his shoulders realising that he had lost all control over the situation.

Joe suddenly hit on an idea. He fished out their travel permit and slammed it down on the table in front of Speiro.

'Look at this, man. I trust you can read.'

'Of course,' he said defiantly and started from the beginning of the typed document. But almost immediately, his eyes were drawn to the handwritten note at the bottom with Lenin's signature. A muted but audible gasp escaped from his lips.

Joe noticed it. 'This is the man whose wishes you are defying,' he said.

Speiro seemed to enter into a trance. Joe remained silent but knew that his hunch had been right. The mere sight of his great hero's signature had sent the poor man into a spin.

Several seconds had passed before Speiro suddenly decided to act speedily and decisively. He grabbed Joe's arm and manhandled him forcefully out of the room and onto the carriage platform which was now swarming with rebels. The sight of their leader, arm in arm with Joe surprised and confused them, and caused an immediate lull in the shouting. Seconds later, it became an almost silent crowd that was addressed by Speiro.

He explained in some detail how they had all been subjected to mischievous rumours and ended with a dramatic display of friendship with Joe and George, shaking hands vigorously with both of them. He went on to explain, in a manner cunningly designed to reflect a degree of glory on himself, how the two men were carrying out important work for Vladimir Lenin himself.

Undoubtedly, there were still dissatisfied elements, some of whom hung around wearily continuing to chant their vicious slogans, but the great threat was over.

The following day, the incident accelerated a meeting with Antonov who turned out to be receptive to the possibility of some form of local treaty. However, other pressing matters demanded his attention and the two men were referred to his deputy in Odessa, which became the next destination for Carriage 451.

Dr Rakovsky proved to be a happy referral. Erudite and highly educated, Joe found him very approachable and open to the notion of such a treaty. After almost three days of tense negotiations, a draft was signed which included deliveries of much-needed food to Rumania and an exchange of prisoners. It was a jubilant Joe who returned to Jassy on the following day. But his high spirits were soon dispelled as George sought him out clutching a new set of orders.

'I'm needed up north, Joe. It seems Lenin's moved the Bolshevik HQ to the Kremlin. London wants me to go to Moscow.'

'It doesn't surprise me, George. You're probably a bit wasted out here in the sticks. My God, I'll miss you though.'

George snorted. 'And I don't know how I'll manage without you,' he paused briefly. 'We made a good partnership, eh?'

'We did indeed, George.'

'Anyway, I'm just grabbing my things and then I'm off.'

'Right. Keep in touch, George. And look after yourself.'

The two looked into each other's eyes. 'Give us a hug then,' said Joe.

They hugged their farewells and George was gone.

But the enemy was now at the gates. German and Austrian forces surrounded the city and King Ferdinand fled to the safety of the south, leaving his wife to turn out the lights. All Allied Missions were required to leave Rumania and, on the sad rainy evening of departure, Queen Marie insisted on saying farewell to each of their leaders. The last to depart was General Berthelot of the French Mission, leaving Marie sitting alone in the reception hall in floods of tears at the thought of the coming occupation. Suddenly, she perceived a shadow at the doorway followed by Joe, soaked to the skin.

'Have you come to see me?' she croaked, dabbing a handkerchief to her eyes.

159

Joe shook his head and answered quietly, 'No. I have come to help you. And my God, Marie, do you need some help?'

This set her weeping once again and he took her in his arms until her sobs gradually died away. They talked for several hours that night and she later wrote in her diary of an 'irresistible sympathy' that had arisen between them.

'We understood each other from the first moment we clasped hands, as though we had never been strangers,' she wrote. 'I tried to let myself be steeled by the man's relentless energy, tried to absorb some of the quiet force that emanated from him. And when he left me and I said that everyone was forsaking me he answered very quietly '…but I won't, and the grip of his hand was as strong as iron.'

They talked well into the small hours, with all her fears and disappointments pouring out of her. Almost alone, she had fought like a wildcat against the appalling peace conditions to be enforced by the occupying forces. These included turning over Rumania's oil to an Austro-German company for ninety years and all its food for nine years, effectively reducing her subjects to a condition of slavery. This, they had stated, would set out a model for all future treaties. Protests on its severity were countered with, 'If you think they are harsh, wait until you see what we have in mind for France and England.'

Her stand against the King and his new puppet Cabinet's acceptance of the terms was applauded by her cousin, King George V, and by the allied press with such headlines as, 'Marie, Queen of Rumania, beloved of her people, refuses to recognise the peace treaty between her little country and Germany.'

But now she felt very much alone. Mentally estranged from her husband and with little local support, she decided to take her daughter to her house in the country. Here, she was soon to be joined by her new friend, Joe Boyle.

Chapter 18

1918. Spring was in the air. But it brought little cheer for the residents of Rumania, the majority of whom were suffering under the harsh occupation of Austro/German forces. Queen Marie could not bear to see her people so mistreated and decided to leave Jassy.

Several years earlier, the King had allowed her to purchase a small dilapidated cottage within the forests of Sinai which she had lovingly restored as a country retreat. Within its sizable garden, she had specified a wooden treehouse to be constructed, perched amongst several giant pine trees. Comprising just two rooms, along with a small kitchen and bathroom, it was approached by a high-level walkway leading to a wooden platform from which a drawbridge led to the front door. From here the bridge could be lifted to provide total privacy, and it was in this unlikely spot that Marie and Joe drew up a raft of schemes to relieve some of the sufferings of her people. Surrounded by maps, they spent their days telephoning and writing letters, drawing up lists of suppliers of food and medical supplies. Some days, Marie would leave Joe to continue alone while she journeyed to one of the hospitals to give succour to the many fallen soldiers.

One day, they decided to have a break and headed off into the hills with a picnic. They discovered that they shared a love of nature and the countryside, Joe had spent many happy hours exploring the flora and fauna of the wilds of Alaska and Marie had herself designed several of the Palace gardens. They walked and talked for many hours that day, Marie learning for the first time that Joe was married. Back in their house by the Yukon River, he hadn't seen the family for nearly a year, although he wrote to them all regularly. She had frequently wondered about his private life. Whilst he was not handsome in a classical sense, his craggy face perfectly matched his powerful frame. But above all, she loved the strength of his character that shone through whatever he was doing or saying, always determined to do what he felt was right at whatever cost to himself.

Marie had endured a dreadful marriage to Ferdinand. He was insecure, manipulative, unattractive and a poor lover. For her part, she was a lively extrovert, intelligent, beautiful and passionate. This led to a series of affairs which became common knowledge but were generally forgiven because of her great popularity.

The following week, Marie took Joe to her favourite place, a clearing deep inside the woods with a series of waterfalls cascading into a pool. It was decorated with an abundance of wildflowers, including orange lilies which were to become the couple's favourites.

In this piece of paradise, it was almost inevitable that they would become lovers. Almost as soon as they arrived, Joe had taken her in his arms and kissed her. She made no move to resist and the kisses became even more passionate until they fell together on a mossy bank amongst the lilies.

Such blissful moments are rarely left unrepeated, and their affair continued in stolen moments, and Carriage 451 was happy to play its part. Together, they took her on tours of neighbouring Bessarabia seeking relief provisions where the added weight of Marie's presence was particularly useful. Throughout the ages, Royalty has found myriad ways of conducting clandestine affairs, and Marie was no exception. For popular consumption, she always travelled on 451 with a friend as a chaperone. But immediately after supper, Ivan would disappear into his minuscule cabin off the kitchen. Many years ago, he had taught himself to read and Marie, who got to know the man well, made sure that she brought him a plentiful supply of books.

But this cosy relationship was suddenly interrupted by a new mission for Joe Boyle. The Rumanian government dithered for weeks over the terms of the treaty Joe had negotiated, but time was now running out with the Crimea soon to be handed over unopposed to the Central Powers. Joe was asked to travel immediately to Odessa to sign the treaty with Dr Rakovsky. The train being considered too slow and unpredictable, Joe clambered aboard a small two-seater plane left by General Berthelot for the Queen's use. With Dr Rakovsky preoccupied with the approaching enemy, terms were agreed in short order and, apart from a few photographs, the treaty was signed with little ceremony.

But as he prepared to fly back, a distraught elderly lady called at his hotel with a tale of woe that demanded his immediate attention. Before he had left, Queen Marie tasked him with ensuring the safety of 70 Rumanian dignitaries being held in Odessa's Turma prison. The group consisted of some noblemen, retired generals and admirals, most of them being old men. As part of the treaty, they were to be exchanged for all captured Russian soldiers and expected to be taken to Rumania by train the following morning. But now, Mrs Ethel Pantazzi, the wife of one of the hostages, stood in front of the mysterious Colonel Boyle who she had been told would be in charge of the following day's prisoner exchange. And she had a very different story to tell.

Not herself one of the prisoners, she had been looking after their affairs and in the course of her visits had befriended one of the more

164

sympathetic prison guards. He had woken her that morning with an insistent telephone call. 'Two hours ago, the prison was taken over by a violent load of scum,' he had whispered, clearly fearful for his safety. 'They are thugs, and they're threatening to take the prisoners away - I think to the port, not the station. You should be worried for their safety.'

Joe dressed rapidly and together they ran down to the waterfront. Sure enough, prisoners were being roughly herded onto the steamship, *Imperator Trajan*. At the gangway, Mrs Pantazzi spotted the local Prisons Commissioner who Mrs Pantazzi had considered kind and humane. He was arguing and gesticulating as Joe approached, but who had to wait until Mrs Pantazzi caught up to translate for him.

'He says that Rakovsky has no intention of releasing the prisoners. He believes such a collection of dignitaries would be more valuable if they were ransomed for money, and that puts them in mortal danger. Rakovsky himself left yesterday evening, taking all the prisoners' valuables.'

Joe could not believe what he was hearing. He had judged Rakovsky to be an honourable man, but now he was breaking the terms of the treaty he had just signed. He leapt into action.

'Ask him who is their leader. We have to stop this.'

Mrs Pantazzi translated, 'His name is Dichescu, and he's over in the *Stefan-cel-Mare*. Over there!' She pointed it out. 'It's the Royal Yacht. They've requisitioned it for their headquarters.'

'Come on, both of you.' Joe was getting angrier by the minute.

Dichescu proved to be a very different man from the cultured Rakovsky, looking and smelling as if he had just emerged from cleaning the bilges. However, although constantly fidgeting and looking over his shoulder, he did listen to Joe's demand that the prisoners be handed over to him under the treaty. He was told firmly that, without an orderly exchange, he would be directly responsible for the lives of 400 Russian prisoners being put at risk.

With no positive response, Joe's anger rose to new heights. He was a terrifying sight and Dichescu sought to control a quaking voice, 'I know nothing of this treaty. My orders come directly from Dr Rakovsky.'

Joe thumped the table with such force that he saw Mrs Pantazzi jump. 'You are not to sail with these poor old men,' he bellowed, barely managing to resist an overwhelming urge to tug at the earrings that dripped from Dichescu's sticking-out ears.

The poor man remained silent for a few seconds, then said, 'If I release them, will you take full responsibility?'

'I will,' Joe assured him. 'I want them paraded on the quayside. Now!'

'I'll try,' Dichescu muttered weakly and scampered on deck to escape the scrutiny of Joe's penetrating eyes.

When they arrived on deck, Dichescu was already shouting orders. Some of his men were beginning to shepherd the exhausted prisoners onto the quayside, but the armed guards by the gangway prevented them from going ashore. Joe started to shout orders to them, translated by the doughty Mrs Pantazzi who was still trotting at his side.

About twenty made it to the shore and some of the younger ones started sprinting to safety. This enraged the guards who opened fire and two men were seen to fall sprawling onto the concrete. A few made it to the comparative safety of the town, but the remainder stopped still with their arms above their heads and were ushered roughly back on board.

166

Dichescu had regained some of his courage and ordered the sailors to cast off. A well-meaning stoker took Mrs Pantazzi aside and urged her to leave the ship. 'Nobody on this ship will survive,' he asserted.

'You should go, Madam,' agreed Joe as she hesitated. 'Thanks for all your help. I will take over now. I am going with them.'

As she stepped onto the gangway, she turned to Joe. 'You'll look after them, won't you,' she pleaded. Joe simply nodded with a reassuring smile.

As the *Trajan* steamed out of the harbour, a large sedan pulled up sharply on the dockside, full of German officers. It was an advance party of the unopposed troops set to occupy the town on the morrow, but all they could do was watch the ship steam out of sight. On board, the Bolshevik gang proceeded to lock all sixty or so prisoners into one large room, along with Joe Boyle. It was going to be a most uncomfortable journey and Joe noted that the sun was beginning to set behind them. They were travelling east - away from Rumania.

Joe was unable to gain any concessions from their guards who were a harsh, embittered band of sailors. The only food they provided was half a dozen tins of cabbage thrown into the cabin. But at least they had not yet been shot or thrown overboard, presumably because they were of value as hostages only if they were kept alive. After three miserable days battling against stormy seas, they were allowed out and shepherded ashore in the Crimean town of Feodosiya. Ducking and diving between White Russians and Bolsheviks who were fighting in the streets, the prisoners were led to a large unoccupied building where Dichescu announced that he was awaiting further orders. He pointed to some bales of hay in one corner saying, 'Sort yourselves out some straw for your bedding,' translated by Commander Pantazzi who had taken over the task from his wife.

There were no locks to the building, but the entrance was continuously manned by armed guards. Joe decided to put them to the test and moved to leave the building. They stopped him firmly, threatening with their guns, whereupon he demanded to speak with Dichescu to explain that he was not one of his prisoners. When he arrived, clearly fearful of the Colonel, he reluctantly told his guards to let him through. Once in the town, Joe sought out the British Vice-Consul and sent a stream of situation reports.

A couple of days later, Joe heard some very unsettling news. A member of the ship's crew sought him out to tell him that hostage negotiations had floundered and Dichescu had been replaced by a more senior member of the revolutionary guards to oversee the disposal of the prisoners. They were to be marched into an old ammunition shed where fuses had already been laid to blow it up, all to be blamed as an accident. Joe realised that he must devise an immediate escape plan.

He paid another visit to the Vice-Consul and together they struck a deal with the captain of an old steamship, the SS *Chernamor,* to take them all to Sevastopol. All that stood in the way were the armed guards, a task Joe reserved for himself.

But a further nasty shock awaited him when he returned to their makeshift prison. As he opened the door, he was confronted with a face he knew. It took less than a second to place, and his heart slumped to his boots. A name followed almost immediately and fell reluctantly from his lips, 'Krylenko.'

The scene of Dukhonin's murder came into his mind in stark detail. If Rakovsky was still in charge, he could not have chosen a better man to kill off the prisoners.

But Krylenko too was thrown by the confrontation, although he could not immediately place Joe. Finally, it came to him - that weird English Colonel who had stood up to him at Stavka. Could he mean trouble?

'I remember you,' he said softly. Pantazzi had been hovering and now translated for Joe.

'And I remember you - unfortunately.'

'Where have you been? Who let you out?' Krylenko demanded roughly.

'I am not one of your Rumanian prisoners, Krylenko. The Queen of Rumania asked me to look after them - to make sure they are well treated before they are exchanged under the treaty with the four hundred Russian prisoners.'

'What treaty?' Krylenko sneered.

'The one I signed with Dr Rakovsky only last week.' Joe moved towards his gear.

'Don't move!' shouted Krylenko, and his hand went to the revolver at his side.

'I have a copy of the treaty in my briefcase. I can show you the clause.'

'I'm not interested,' the wretched man said. 'I have my orders.'

'But...' Joe started.

'Shut the fuck up,' shouted Krylenko, his face only inches from Joe's. 'I will not listen to another word.'

With that, he turned to his guards and told them to treat Joe as one of the prisoners, not to let him out again. He then turned to Commander Pantazzi, 'Tell your fellow prisoners that tomorrow morning we will be moving them to some better quarters.'

Joe reasoned that any further talk would be useless. The man had closed his mind and tomorrow they would all be killed. He must act tonight.

Only some two hundred yards away, The *Imperator Trajan* still housed the guards and Joe was certain that Krylenko would also sleep in its comparative comfort. However, at least two of his heavily armed thugs would always remain on guard, changed every two or three hours.

As night fell, Joe outlined his plan to the prisoners telling them to prepare for sleep as usual, but to be ready to leave at a moment's notice. A couple of hours into the night, he got up and dressed, all the time watched with curiosity by the two guards. As Joe moved casually toward the exit, they grew increasingly twitchy, raising their rifles and gesticulating him to return to his bed. Joe indicated that he couldn't sleep, which annoyed the two men who started shouting angrily in Russian. But a fragmented conversation had been forced on them and Joe continued to move up close to them.

With Joe's lifelong boxing experience and immense physical strength, the two men stood no chance. They simply never saw it coming - just two thumping punches that laid both of them out cold.

Now awake, a couple of the prisoners helped Joe secure the two guards and assemble the rest of their party. Quietly, Joe opened the door to find the town fast asleep. Feeling rather like Moses, he led his trusty band of old men through empty streets down to the quayside.

But as they rounded the last building, Joe was shocked to find that the *Trajan* had its own two guards who immediately threatened with their rifles and shouted for them to move back. In no time, Krylenko arrived and smiled as he took charge, approaching Joe with a gun in his hand.

'I forget your name, Colonel', he said, and then appeared to enter a short trance. Suddenly, he turned to the two guards who had their rifles trained on Joe.

'Drop your rifles,' he barked. Both hesitated, but the younger one then set his gun down on the quayside. The older man thought a moment longer but then turned his aim toward Krylenko.

A shot rang out and everyone ducked involuntarily. A surprised look and a neat round hole appeared in the centre of the older guard's face and he crumpled into an untidy heap on the concrete.

Krylenko turned to his other guards who were hovering on the ship's side. 'All of you, go below,' he ordered, 'and leave your rifles on the gangplank.'

Bewildered, but shocked at what they had just witnessed, they reluctantly complied with their boss's command.

'I will defend to my death all the principles that Comrade Lenin stands for. Yes, I am a Revolutionary - a Bolshevik if you like. But that doesn't make me a criminal,' he paused for a moment before continuing, 'I believe I said it to you once before, Colonel - just bugger off, and take that motley crew with you.'

Joe didn't need a second offer. He said nothing, but stepped forward and gave Krylenko's shoulder a gentle squeeze. Ten minutes later, the *Chernamor* slipped quietly out of the port.

But the successful escape was far from the end of their troubles. The *Chernamor* was a leaky, coal-burning wreck of a ship that was forced by rough seas to sail dangerously close to the shore. After a couple of uncomfortable days, it chugged into Sevastopol - and straight into the arms of the occupying German Army.

Following his usual practice, Joe immediately went to the top and demanded to see the General in charge to explain his mission. Within the hour, he was amazed to find himself standing before the wily Field Marshal Von Mackensen who must have been intrigued by the morning report of an odd band of old men travelling in a rustbucket, apparently being led by a British army officer. Nicknamed 'the last Hussar', this was the man who, only a few months earlier, had led the Central Powers' triumphant victory parade in Bucharest.

Joe gave him a summary of his background and explained that he was on a mercy mission, attempting to lead this collection of old men to freedom. Mackensen was inclined to sympathise and issued a safe pass but with one strange condition.

'I accept that you are engaged in a mission devoid of any act of war. This being the case, you will please exchange your army uniform for civilian clothes.' Apart from the golden Yukon signs on his jacket lapels, Joe's uniform was almost identical to that of a British officer and therefore probably repugnant to the great architect of Germany's defeat of Rumania.

Joe stood ramrod erect. He was practically sewn into his unique uniform and was rarely seen out of it. 'Field Marshal,' he began. 'No German living will compel me to take off my uniform. I carry a single-action Colt and am a man of my word. I will drill a hole in the first

German, be he General or private, who lays violent hands on me.'
These were the words as reported, but it was the posture rather than the
actual words that were so typical of Joseph Boyle.

Those standing around the two men drew in their breath.
Mackensen puffed out his chest as he too drew breath, apparently fit to
explode. But after a few seconds, his face cracked open into a broad
grin, and then a loud laugh. 'I do have to admire your guts, Colonel. I
have accepted your mission as an act of mercy, so I suppose clothing is
immaterial. Good luck to you, Sir.'

True to his word, he organised safe passage for their ramshackle
old boat to travel on to Sulina, a railhead at the mouth of the Danube.
Joe telegraphed the arrangements to the Rumanian Prime Minister and
the *Chernamor* set off on what was almost certain to be its final journey.

Very early the following morning, they all left on a very special train
laid on by Queen Marie for the last leg of their tortuous journey. Having
survived the terrors of the criminal gang, the party was now faced with a
train ordered by Royalty to arrive in Jassy in time for lunch. They
cowered in terror as it sped along at breakneck speed, the train
constantly threatening to jump the track.

The Rumanian dignitaries occupied a couple of elegant first-class
carriages and were served coffee and cakes. But Joe was delighted to
sink back into the comforts of Carriage 451, which Marie had insisted be
hitched to the rear of the train, and enjoyed his favourite breakfast
served by a chirpy Ivan. He was very touched when, at some point
during the journey, each of the old men braved the violent motions of the
train to thank him and spend some time with him.

173

When the train finally arrived, they were greeted by wildly cheering crowds. With the defeated country in deep depression, this was a rare moment of hope and, for a second time in Jassy station, Joe was given a hero's welcome. There were unashamed tears from Marie as her husband awarded him the Grand Cross of the Star of Rumania, and the following morning the erstwhile "King of the Klondike" had gained a new title when the newspapers detailed his deeds and hailed him as 'The Saviour of Rumania'.

Marie was so happy to have Joe back alive and successful in his mission. His popularity boosted the couple's famine relief efforts but at the same time hampered their intimacy, privacy becoming a scarce commodity. Carriage 451 was happy to assist in this and made many sorties into the wilds of Bessarabia.

Whilst Joe was away, Marie had moved to Peles, a fairy-tale castle deep in the Carpathian mountains. Life returned to a familiar routine, with long hours spent bettering the lives of citizens in a whole variety of ways. But Joe soon began to feel isolated, removed from the larger perspective of world events, and the war in particular. His work introduced him to many well-connected and influential people and he began to piece together a network of informants. Very soon he was able to resume passing useful information to London.

Chapter 19

At the Foreign Office, a timid knock at the door arouses Coldwell from a reverie. 'Come,' he shouts.

Just the face of his secretary appears around the door. 'There's a Damian Parmentier to see you, Sir. He hasn't got an appointment, but says he knows you.' Then, with a glance over her shoulder, she adds in a whisper, 'I believe he's MI6, Sir.'

'That is true, Betty. No need to whisper. It's not a state secret. Show him in, will you.'

The newly appointed second-in-command of external Military Intelligence is the best part of a generation younger than Coldwell, but he is from the same mould and they have always got along together well enough.

'Do sit down, Damian. To what do we owe this pleasure?'

'Bit awkward actually, Bob.' A good-looking man, sandy-haired and with millions of freckles, Parmentier possesses a slight misalignment in his eyes and you are never quite sure if he is looking at you. 'Do you recall the name, Joseph Boyle?'

'I certainly do. We haven't been having so many complaints about him over the last few months, but he's not one of ours anyway. We've been trying to get the Canadians to reel him in.'

'That's the man. And I gather the Foreign Office has been adding its weight to get the man removed.' He clears his throat nervously before continuing, 'trouble is, he's one of our best assets in Europe right now.'

'Good heavens, really?'

'Well, he has exceeded his original brief, it's true. But he's made several important contacts and he's there, on the ground, where he can see and put into action all sorts of ways to assist the war effort.' He shrugged his shoulders. 'He's just using his loaf and his considerable skills. We've had reports from one of our best agents who's been working with him, and he's also very impressed with the man - claims they've been doing great things together. He's had head-to-head meetings with both Joffe and Lenin for Christ's sake. And now we hear that he's met with Joseph Stalin and sent in a report that their government is in course of being rehoused in Moscow.'

'Good heavens,' exclaimed Coldwell. 'What's he up to at the moment?'

'Well, without going into details, he seems to have turned his attention to poor old Rumania, which is being so appallingly treated by the occupying forces. Apparently, he's wormed his way into the affections of the Queen and at the same time set himself up with his own little spy ring.

'That's amazing. Unbelievable really.'

'I know. We had to check it all out because he requested some funds to run these activities. And it's all true. General Berthelot - he's head of the French mission in Rumania - confirmed it all for us. We're subbing to the tune of £10M, and the French are giving him a similar amount.'

'Sounds like the bloke deserves a medal, not a bollocking.'

Parmentier smiles. 'Maybe he'll get one, Bob - after the war.'

'Anyway, what I came to ask is for you to lay off him. He seems to be doing a good job, so just let him be, eh.'

'Willingly. I'll be more than happy to rid myself of his file. I just didn't expect to do so in this manner.'

'Good man,' said Parmentier as he got up to leave.

'I'll show you to the front gate, Damian. I could do with some air.'

As spring moved slowly into summer, so did the course of the war begin to turn. With the new Bolshevik government withdrawing from the conflict, Germany was able to consolidate its armies, but this was more than matched by the deployment of American forces and equipment. Victory for the Allies became only a matter of time.

At Peles Castle, Joe and Marie took advantage of the improved weather with long rides into the mountains on horses from the Royal stables. Their relationship deepened all the time, both being full-blooded individuals who lived life on their own terms. They were aware of the possible penalties for their relationship but sufficiently committed to risk them. Joe was everything that all other men in her life never were, whilst her unique qualities stretched far beyond any woman Joe had ever known.

But in mid-July, Marie's network of royal families began to buzz with the news of the execution of Tsar Nicholas II. It was to be several months before the full horror was revealed - that along with the Tsar, his wife and five children had also been shot and bayoneted to death. The whole barbaric episode spelt out a clear warning to the Russian aristocracy and in particular to the remainder of the Romanov family. Chief among these was the Dowager **Empress Maria Feodorovna,** mother of Tsar Nicholas, who had sometime earlier taken refuge with other family members in the Lividia Palace, the family's principal summer residence in the Crimea.

The British government was equally shocked by the massacre. Maria Feodorovna was doubly blood-related to King George V and a frequent visitor to England. It was almost inevitable that the problem should arrive at Coldwell's desk in the Foreign Office. He found himself immediately called to the office of the Foreign Minister. The King himself had taken a personal interest in the Empress's welfare and had already received support from the Royal Navy. They had agreed to make available HMS Marlborough, a battleship no less, which was soon due to return home from the Black Sea, but all efforts were hampered by the lady's steadfast refusal to leave her country. Did the Department have anyone with local influence that might persuade her otherwise?

'I do know of one chap who could be useful. We've been keeping him in reserve for such an operation. He has a certain influence over Rumanian royalty and they all seem to be connected in some way or another. It's worth a try.'

'OK. See what you can do. Make it a priority, please. And keep me fully posted, will you? I might get a call from Buck House at any time.'

Back in his office, Coldwell pressed a key on his intercom. 'Betty, the file we had on Joe Boyle - we closed it only a few days ago. I trust it hasn't gone to the archives already. I need it again.'

'No. I always keep them back for a while. I'll bring it in.'

Joe was not enthused by Coldwell's telegram. If the good lady wished to remain in her country, what could he do? After all, she must surely be aware of the dangers. But Marie was far more concerned and set herself the task of convincing her namesake to seek at least temporary safety from the Bolshevik assassins. A few days later, her task was hugely assisted by breaking news of the atrocious assassination of five more members of her family, including her cousin, Grand Duchess Elizabeth Feodorovna. Having survived being thrown down a deep mineshaft, they were heard singing hymns whereupon their killers threw down hand grenades and left them all to die in agony.

The Dowager Empress had never publicly accepted that her sons and grandchildren had been murdered. Now in her mid-seventies, and with the announcement of this new atrocity, she finally acknowledged the truth and accepted the British offer.

One evening, she was recounting some early memories of the Empress when Joe's enthusiasm for the project suddenly leapt into overdrive. He recalled his first meeting with the manager of the rail museum in Petrograd. Surely, he had stated that Carriage 451 had once belonged to Empress Maria Feodorovna, even to the extent of her being involved in its design. The notion of showing it to her once again, whilst recounting its wartime adventures, excited him and he lost no time in contacting London to finalise the arrangements.

The German forces were now overstretched and beginning to lose control of occupied territories. Joe had experienced little difficulty in travel within Bessarabia and other neighbouring countries and had acquired a fistful of permits including the pass from Von Mackensen. But he soon discovered that no railway stretched beyond Sevastopol, so it was here that he would marshal the leaving party ready to be picked up by HMS Marlborough.

Joe found a suitable Sevastopol hotel more than a little happy to welcome such a large party, but it was not until they had all arrived that he learned that the total number of the leaving entourage had risen to 70 persons, 6 cats and a canary.

In the afternoon, Joe was formally introduced to many of the leading members of the royal family who were leaving for England. After thanking Joe for organising the exodus, formality was dropped a trifle and Empress Maria took Joe aside.

'I'm told you have a surprise for me, Mr Boyle,' she said in very passable English.

'I do, Ma'am. I have a coach waiting outside to take us to the station.'

'My goodness, Sir. Where are you taking me?' she demanded with a twinkle in her eye. 'I have heard of your reputation and wonder whether I might need a chaperone. My friend here, Duchess Xenia. Can she come along?'

'By all means,' Joe agreed with a bow of acknowledgement to the Duchess. He let pass the slightly worrying remark about his reputation. 'Let's go.'

On entering the station, the Empress did not at first notice her carriage. Then, she suddenly shrieked with joy.

'Ivan,' she shouted.

Her steward was standing bolt upright at the carriage entrance, dressed in his colourful dress uniform.

'And my old carriage.' She shouted, adding, 'What a treat!'

Ivan bowed deeply as she approached and spoke to him for several minutes. She then turned to a beaming Joe and said, 'Thank you so much, Mr Boyle. I have such happy memories of this carriage. May we go onboard?'

'By all means, Ma'am.' He took her proffered gloved hand to help her climb the steep steps where she took her friend on a complete tour, stopping from time to time to tell a story of some family event. Finally, they joined Joe in the living room and settled down to a cup of tea and a plate of Ivan's irresistible cakes, which she well remembered.

Joe started on his history of Carriage 451's war. He had decided to stick to the rescue of the Rumanian crown jewels, feeling sure that the Empress would appreciate the justice of their return. She listened intently, making the occasional comment. At the point when Joe hid the jewels in Ivan's kitchen, she told Xenia of the time that her children had been saved in the same hiding place. It was a good quarter of an hour before Joe described their tumultuous reception in Jassy when both ladies applauded wildly.

In the evening, Joe hosted a leaving party opening with a typical Joe Boyle address. He began by acknowledging the heartbreak of leaving the country of one's birth, but then looked forward to the exciting prospects of a new start in a land free of the Red Terror which was beginning to pervade the whole of Russia. Joe's use of this expression was interesting. It was new to members of his audience, although each could of course guess its meaning. Opposition to his regime had been increasing over several months and was approaching the point of counter-revolution. Along with peasant uprisings, White Brigades had been formed to fight against the Bolsheviks, infuriating their leader who had 100 peasants executed as a public deterrent. Fanya Kaplan's subsequent brave attempt on Lenin's life had failed, triggering him to call for a 'ruthless mass terror' which was now about to begin in all its horrors. Whether Joe had seen or heard the **expression** "Red **Terror**" will never be known, but it could possibly have been born in this well-reported speech. However this may be, it was enthusiastically taken up by the world's press.

He concluded by wishing them all the best of luck for their coming adventure and introduced the captain of the mighty vessel they would be joining in the morning.

'I now pass on to you, Sir, the responsibility for delivering these good people to Britain. May they prosper in their new land until, in the bright sunshine of the coming world peace, their mother country once again becomes a stable and safe place for their return.'

Queen Marie gave Joe a joyous welcome home, oblivious to the disaster that was about to strike. As peace moved ever closer, their work was by no means over and Joe would spend many hours away from Peles Castle. On one expedition into Bessarabia, he was travelling in Marie's light aeroplane when the Rumanian pilot felt the fragile frame begin to vibrate wildly. Looking over his shoulder into the rear cockpit, he could see his passenger waving wildly and trying to speak, but with a face livid and distorted. He was an experienced pilot and, realising that something was seriously wrong, instantly headed the plane down towards the nearest town he could see through his goggles. It turned out to be Kishineff, the capital of Bessarabia, which sported a modern hospital, where it was soon established that the Saviour of Rumania had suffered a stroke in mid-air.

Although he was in good hands now, his life hung in the balance for several days. When he did eventually emerge from the fog, he immediately railed against what he found. His tongue was thick and heavy, and the right side of his face was frozen. He attempted to speak, but could only mumble incoherently. Thrashing around in anguish, he fought with the nursing staff as he attempted to get out of bed. But his leg and the whole of his right side were paralysed, and he fell back into the pillows exhausted.

'I felt my heart die within me,' wrote Marie when she heard the news.' She immediately sent her personal physician to assist in his treatment, who found that the local doctors had told their patient that any hope of becoming whole again was utterly hopeless.

But these good people did not know Joe Boyle.

He spent hour after hour straightening the stricken side of his face with his fingers in front of a hand mirror until it became almost normal once again. He then called for a full-length mirror which was hung on the wall and every morning he exercised his lame arm and leg in front of it, forcing them to function properly. After only six weeks, he was pronounced fit enough to be moved.

Marie was determined to take charge of his recuperation. Joe asked to be housed in one of the cottages in the castle grounds, and Marie organised its conversion to better accommodate his needs. Life soon developed into a pattern. Each morning, Marie joined her hero for breakfast after which, weather permitting, they took the children for a drive into the countryside for a picnic. This was exactly what Joe's body needed, and much of his strength and lust for life gradually began to return. He took an increasing interest in Marie's work and ranged far and wide seeking new supplies of food and medicine. He secured $25 million in loans from Canada and promises of nine cargo ships of food from the USA.

In recognition, Marie bestowed upon him the very personal Order of Maria Regina. When the German surrender was signed in November, he was decorated with the Croix de Guerre by General Berthelot and, to the vexation of the Foreign Office, he received the Distinguished Service Order in the King's 1919 birthday honours list.

In addition, King Ferdinand and Marie granted him a title, the Duke of Jassy, which permitted Marie to seat him closer to her at formal functions and later to advise her at the Paris Peace Conference. The Rumanian delegation led by Bratiano was floundering miserably in their negotiations and it was only through Queen Marie's intervention behind the scenes that a good settlement was secured with Rumania remaining intact, and even expanded by the addition of Bessarabia.

It was inevitable that there would be a backlash against so much power being wielded by a foreigner, and Joe's activities came under criticism from Rumanian political circles. It became inevitable that Joe would be forced to leave the country which he did without an argument. But in a wistfully resigned tone, he wrote to Marie, 'I want you to be happy. That's all I know these days.'

Over the next few years, Joe's health deteriorated rapidly. His face became gaunt and, towards the end, his powerful frame withered to less than six stone. Eventually, at the beginning of 1923, he moved to London to rest and recuperate, settling in a small room in the house of Teddy Bredenberg, his old friend from the Yukon days.

The last couple of months of Joe's life passed happily enough. He had the company of his dear friend and his three young boys who he took to the cinema and regaled with tales of all his exploits.

One morning, he failed to wake up.

Teddy arranged a simple but well-attended funeral. His estranged son, Joe Jr., came over from Canada and George Hill joined the mourners, as did a gentleman from the Foreign Office. But pressing state duties precluded Queen Marie's presence on the day, and it was some time before she marked her stamp on his burial site. She arranged for the headstone to be replaced by an ancient rough stone cross that she had shipped from Rumania and a large slab of granite to cover his grave. In the lower right corner was engraved the Insignia of the Order of Maria Regina and at the foot of the slab were words from one of Boyle's favourite poems by Robert Service selected by Marie as his eternal epitaph:

> *"A man with the heart of a Viking*
> *and the simple faith of a child."*

Later, on her first visit, she also installed a stone urn to hold the flowers she had brought and planted around the gravestone some tendrils of ivy she had taken from the Rumanian countryside in which they had spent such happy hours. And every year until she died just before the outbreak of World War II, a veiled figure dressed in black, would visit the grave, trim back the ivy, lay a large spray of orange lilies and kneel for a while, gently weeping.

At the funeral, Teddy read out parts of a 12-page letter she had written to him.

'He had come to me in my hour of deepest distress, all strength and honour. And I was something of a miracle in his life when he had his stroke. I was the haven in which he anchored for a while...

For me, he is not dead. He was so big, he belonged absolutely to nature. He is in the trees, in the sky, in the sea, in the sun and the wind, he is in the freshness of the early morning and the silence of night, and the stars seem to watch me with his eyes and the clouds seem to bring me messages from that great heart that was mine.'

Epilogue

Carriage 451 survived Joe Boyle by only a few months. The reconstruction of Europe was gathering speed and steel was in great demand. In Petrograd, renamed Leningrad just five days after the death of Lenin, the manager of the railway museum made tentative efforts to rehouse her but could not match her scrap value.

And so, one sunny morning, she made her final journey, drawn by a utility engine into the heart of the mighty Slavik breakers yards in Odessa. Her noble lineage was treated with due respect at first. Furnishings and articles of any value were carefully removed, catalogued and entered into the next on-site auction. Wood panelling was removed and seats unbolted, all taken away to be restored and put up for sale. The panels of armour plating were carefully stripped from the carriage frame. Made of toughened steel they were to be offered to selected military customers.

Then the slaughter began as giant claws grabbed what was left of the carriage. It was lifted up and crashed to the ground. Lifted, shaken and dropped to the ground once again. Very soon, wheels, whole bogies, doors, and roof sections began to fly off. Later, the chassis cracked and the carriage slowly folded in two. The torture stopped for a while as all the metal that had been released was collected and taken to the smelting sheds.

She sighed and groaned as she continued to fall apart and very soon became nothing more than a small footnote in history.

Printed in Great Britain
by Amazon

31952641R00106